I0618430

ROOSEVELT STREET
A
NOVEL
BY
RICHARD E. MOUSSEAU

MOOSE HIDE BOOKS
imprint of
MOOSE ENTERPRISE PUBLISHING
PRINCE TOWNSHIP
ONTARIO, CANADA

cover illustration by Richard Mousseau

ROOSEVELT STREET
Copyright April 1998
by
RICHARD E. MOUSSEAU

Published September 1, 1999
by

MOOSE HIDE BOOKS
imprint of
MOOSE ENTERPRISE PUBLISHING
684 WALLS ROAD
PRINCE TOWNSHIP
ONTARIO, CANADA
P6A 6K4
web site www.moosehidebooks.com

NO VENTURE UNATTAINABLE

THIS BOOK IS AN AUTOBIOGRAPHY OF THE AUTHOR'S LIFE WHILE LIVING ON ROOSEVELT STREET. THIS COLLECTION OF STORIES ARE TRUE TO THE BEST OF THE AUTHOR'S MEMORY. TIMES AND EVENTS MAY SLIGHTLY DIFFER THAN ANOTHER'S RECOLLECTION. THESE STORIES ARE GIVEN WITH THE GREATEST AMOUNT OF RESPECT TO THE PEOPLE OF ROOSEVELT STREET. THERE IS NO MALICIOUS INTENT TO THOSE LIVING OR DECEASED. CREATIVE NARRATIVE AND SLIGHT EXAGGERATION IS USED TO ENHANCE THE STORY LINES.

CREATED IN CANADA

Library and Archives Canada Cataloguing in Publication

Mousseau, Richard E., author
    Roosevelt Street / Richard Mousseau

ISBN 978-0-968490-93-8 (PBK).—ISBN 978-1-927393-44-4 (PDF)

1. Mousseau, Richard E.–Childhood and youth.
2. Authors, Canadian (English)-- 20th century–Biography.

   I. Title.

PS8576.0977Z53 1999 C818'.5409   C99-900643-6
PR9199.3.M677Z476 1999
PS8576.O977R655 2017   C813'.54 C2017-901665-2

ROOSEVELT STREET

ROOSEVELT STREET
CHAPTER 1
ROOSEVELT STREET

Roosevelt Street, it was just a name of a street in Brookfield subdivision in the township of Korah. Sault Ste. Marie was just a stones' throw away from the rural township. In the nineteen fifties, the Sault had a growing population of about sixty-two thousand people.

On Roosevelt Street, the street in question, the houses were built by veterans of world war two. Kids, kids galore were coming out of the woodwork. Uncommon was to have a household with a meager one or two children.

Remember now that it has been a good eleven years since the war was over. A prosperous time had now begun. Those lucky enough to have survived the war were putting their lives in order. Most young men on Roosevelt Street had landed secure jobs at a local steel mill. Algoma Steel was in the heart of the city producing steel that was building up the Canadian economy. At the time this meant nothing to the kids of Roosevelt Street.

Two-story homes with asphalt base shingles on the walls that looked like brick. Bungalow homes with slate shingle sidings. A few homes had pine lapped boards painted white. During the dry months, the families paid a few dollars to have old oil poured onto the gravel road to cut down on the dust. Deep ditches lined each side of the street. This was a great place to play cowboys ambushing other neighborhood kids. Lawns were beginning to grow as the families slowly began sprucing up their places.

Very few fences enclosed people's properties. It seemed that any kid was free to travel up one side and down the other side through back yards and front yards. No one ever complained. If someone decided to start at one end heading to the other there was sure to be a group of kids gathered along the way. It seemed that age or gender did not matter much. Two to four years of age difference was common. Older kids willingly looked after the younger kids.

What and who made up the fabric of the people on this street? The basic fabrics were the needs of people to live together. A life of mediocrity and a world war were the evil, people wanted to leave behind. Good times were ahead. Surnames meant nothing if one was to think back to that time-period. At least the kids did not think so. Kids were kids living and playing together as they grew up, and everyone played with everyone.

Who were these people? Just plain everyday people. Wives stayed home raising their children, husbands that labored hard with their hands. There were no rich people nor were they poor lacking in family love. All of the families seemed to struggle at the same rate.

Roosevelt Street resembled a walking cane running north to south. The cane's hook tied into another street that lead to the main highway at the north end. At the south end was a dead end which ended at a creek. Houses lined both sides of the road. Each house sat on a one-half acre of land with newly planted trees and shrubs taking root. For a quarter of a mile Roosevelt Street ran with Balfour Street crossing at the middle. Asquith street headed east at the bottom end of Roosevelt Street.

A street that was a world unto its own. Some children did not know what their fathers had fought for in world war two. Ahead were adventures in growing up where kids made their own fun in summer, winter, rain or sunshine. What was in the minds of war veterans? What was in the mind of children that seldom asked what their fathers did years before in a darker period of history?

Music arrived on the airwaves, scratches of static came from tiny speakers in radios on kitchen counters. Records turned at revolutions of seventy-eight, thirty-three and a third and the new forty-fives on record player machines. It was the beginning of the electronic age, an age where the invention of television was yet years away. On Roosevelt Street, the first television set did not arrive until nineteen-fifty-five.

Children on Roosevelt Street did not need the distraction of fuzzy figures of black and white on a twelve-inch screen. There were games to be played, adventures to seek out. Simple stories to be left to memories of growing up on Roosevelt Street.

If only to remember the families that lived on the street. Years have passed and memories are misplaced. There was, the Bradley's at the north end, the Corbett's...Redfern, Scott, Seccariccia, Yanni, Turvy, Pelletier, Auger, Corbett, Dewer, Mousseau, Thibodeau, Birch, Barber, McAuley, Watson, Hebert, Smyth, Sullivan, Johnson, Wozny, Guertin, Mathews, Hall, Mousseau, Hartman, Thurston, Potoczny, Bender, McFarling, Clulow, Dennison, Mckenzie, Burns, Marson..., a few have been forgotten in memory.

REMEMBERING
CHAPTER 2
BEST FRIEND

It was Richard's Mom's Aunt's place, the Dewer's two- story house. With a two-year-old child in tow Mom and Dad rented the white house. Mom's aunt and uncle were working up the line. A term meaning working up along the Algoma Central Railway Line near Montreal River.

At two years of age Richard remembered very little of moving into the house. All of the furniture had been moved during the day. So, when everything was ready the family car pulled into the driveway late at night. For a split second, Richard caught a glimpse of the tall white house before the car lights went out. Shadows moved among the familiar furniture in the strange rooms. Comfort of his bed brought sleep to the baby's eyes.

Getting use to one's surroundings takes time. In a child's eye, everything is viewed between two and three feet from the ground. The house was easy to assimilate with, the outside world was a bit different. While riding in the family car or walking on the street with his Mom Richard laid out his new world in his mind.

Richard noticed houses that had children his age. Those were interesting places and worth remembering. Other houses had older kids, not much interest there. There was one house next door the Truvy house. It had red brick but not real red brick, it was made of asphalt sheets made to resemble real brick. This house seemed dark, lights never came on. Richard wondered if anyone lived there.

Summer became fall when slowly the colour of the sky changed and the healthy tree leaves became brightly lit then dulled and died. A slight smell of heat from the wood and coal furnace filtered up through the duct work then through the floor grates on the second floor. Music from the year nineteen-fifty-seven also followed the heat up to the second floor into Richard's room. It was about the time Richard had turned four years old.

From his room, Richard peeked out through the rain spattered bedroom windows. Rain sparkled with reflection from the sporadic lightning. The big dark two-story house next door seemed eerie and haunting. Maybe it just wanted and needed a new family to brighten up the echoing empty rooms.

With the soothing patter of rain on the roof Richard bid the house a goodnight as he laid his head down on a goose-down pillow. In dreams, he recalled that his Mom said that a new family would be moving into the house next door. 'They would be moving in soon' his Mom would answer each day that she was asked by her anxious son.

Anxious was right, for there was a good chance there might be a boy his age moving in right next door. For an anxious kid soon never arrives fast enough.

Soon did arrive that night as Richard dreamed of a possible new best friend. Under the cover of darkness and rain a new family moved into the reddish brick house. For the first time in a long-time, lights shone from the windows. The house was beginning to come alive again. Excitement and wonderment were missed while deep sleep filled Richard's mind.

When the first light of morning arrived through his bedroom window, Richard looked out through sleep incrusted eyes. A grey morning with lingering rain soon would pass as a cool fall day began. Something looked different about the house next door. The house was the same. Nothing different about the red asphalt siding. The dingy windows were the same. Wait, there were curtains on the insides of the window right across from Richard's bedroom window. There was something different but Richard failed to put two and two together.

Mom placed a bowl of hot oatmeal in front of him at the kitchen table. Richard moved the bowl around the grey granite coloured table top. A squeaking sound of plastic against bare legs came from the seat of the chrome chair. To this day that same table is still hanging around the garage, the plastic-covered chairs are gone. With a piece of toast Richard began his ritual of dunking it into his hot oatmeal. It was a lazy dunk until his Mom's words changed his mood.

"Richard, the new family moved into the house next door."

With baited excitement Richard listened as Mom listed the details.

"Mr. and Mrs. Pelletier. They have three girls, Lynn, Joyce and Gail." said Mom, she paused.

"Girls, who needs girls."

Baby sitters, that was what was going through Mom's mind. Richard wanted news of a boy. Was there a boy in this family?

Mom brushed back a strand of brown hair from her eye. Richard watched his Mom stack dishes into the big double porcelain sink. The one he sometimes had to take a bath in. Another dunk of toast into the oatmeal then into his mouth while he anticipated further words from his Mom.

"And I think there is a boy your age."

'She just thinks there is a boy, why does she not know. She knows about the girls.' questionable questions formed in his mind.

Mom turned to face the table. "His name is Mark."

"Is he my age, can I go see him?" Little hands began to move faster. The oatmeal and toast vanished before Mom's eyes. "Can I go see if he is home right now?"

Before Mom was able to explain, that the new neighbors arrived late last night and maybe would be sleeping in this morning, Richard high tailed it up the staircase to his room. At five years of age the once blonde curly hair was turning brown. Baby fat was long gone. His new born baby brother Donald had plenty of baby fat.

With a warm coat and mitts, a toque on his head, feet snug into rubber boots, Richard stood like a statue at the edge of the driveway looking towards the back of the next-door house. Teddy, Richard's mutt of a dog busied itself on an old bone he had saved from three weeks ago.

A freckled face boy bundled up and unable to move as freely as one would wish made his way out of the back door of the red brick house. Squeaking to a closed position, the screen door slapped behind Richard's new best friend. Mark slowly inched his way towards his waiting neighbor. Reddish brown hair poked out from under his cap. A cap with built-in ear muffs. Both boys eyed each other without saying a word. When you are kids there sometimes is no need for introductions or even for an exchange of words.

Teddy looked over towards the two boys standing there doing nothing. If there was no excitement, Teddy decided he should devote his time on the old ham bone. Dogs and kids understand each other. Maybe it is because they are able to look each other directly into each other's eyes and see the innocence and trust.

Moments seemed like minutes. Those silent moments said everything that was required for two boys to understand each other. Feeble rays of sun began to warm the morning air. Life on the ground began to come alive. Mark pointed a mitt-covered finger towards the imaginary property line that separated the two houses. Bending to his knees, Mark began taking a closer look. Richard hunched down beside Mark to investigate a tiny creature.

Mark and Richard watched a slowly moving Daddy-Long-Legs spider make its way along the gravel. It must have seemed like bolder sized gravel to the tiny spider. In silence the two best friends watched in mutual bonding as the spider went about its life in an uncertain world.

REMEMBERING
CHAPTER 3
HANG HIM HIGH

There were good guys and bad guys. In every cowboy show there had to be good guys and bad guys. Playing cowboys on Roosevelt Street was not any different except that everyone wanted to be the good guy. Can you blame a kid for wanting to be like his cowboy hero?

Roy Rogers, Gene Autry, Richard Boone as Paladin, the Lone Ranger and John Wayne were always the good guys. The bad guys never had names to remember. All you would see would be dark figures riding away from Roy Rogers and his horse Trigger. Dust was billowing into the air between black and white static on the tiny television screen. When the dust settled, the bad guy was hauled off to jail while Gene Autry sang a western song.

Good ole days on the street was when the boys got together to have a shoot out. With plastic guns and rifles, some made out of wood, the boys would hide in the ditches, behind houses and under bushes ready to ambush the bad guy. There was a slight problem, everybody was a good guy. You just can not have good guys shooting at good guys. Not a bad guy for blocks around. Not one no-good low-down varmint to send off to jail.

It must have been about the time Richard was six years old. Bart, Billy, Pat, Mark and Terry were also the same age. The other boys that day were a couple of years older. Being a cowboy did not matter. Leading the band of good guys were Francis, Tom and Jerry.

Mark had a real replica of the rifleman's rifle that he would swing around under his arm, sometimes. A double holster like Have-Gun-Will-Travel was what Richard wore low on his hips. Everyone had their own preference of weapons, black revolvers, silver shooters, long rifles. Jerry used a long barrel Wyatt Earp six shooter.

Brothers Tom and Pat relied on wooden rifles that shot real rubber bands. Rubber band rifles were only good at close range when they were able to sneak up on someone. There was always an unwritten rule, a code of the west that all good cowboys abide by. In the midst of a shootout, when bullets are flying and dust is chocking the throat, if someone shouted, "I got you", then you would give the greatest dying performance ever. You had to, how else would they know that they got you.

Second rule was good because after a count of ten you were alive again and fair game for the shooter. Day in and day out this would go on because everyone was a good guy. What this street needed was a bad guy, a stranger, someone from a street over. Someone that had to be the bad guy if he wanted to play on our street. On this hot summer day, a gang of bad guys would be great.

Mark and Richard had been riding and checking out the terrain early this morning. A few dogs had been rounded up and corralled in the north end of the street. One mean old dog, Richard's dog Teddy, was the hardest to wrangle. After just one roping Teddy headed for the hills, probably home to the shade of an apple tree.

These two cowpokes slowly gathered up old buddies and began making their way down the street. Just kids dressed in shirts, jeans, street shoes and imaginations bigger than reality or the street on which they lived.

The north end boys now included Jerry, Mark, Richard, Bart and Pat. They were hungry cowboys when they wandered by ready to raid the McAuley's garden. No time to stop they were on the move. As fast as they arrived, they departed with their pockets filled with sweet peas and long yellow beans. Hot green onions only for the real hardy cowboy.

From the south making their way north another group of good cowboys were having a shootout as they moved from house to house. Walking like the Duke Francis was leading the boys. Francis did not hide behind houses and trees, he stayed in the open and picked off everyone with a fanning of his pistol.

Tom, Terry and Billy dropped with excellent performances of great actors deserving of academy awards.

Like any day for a kid a day lasted forever. A kid could go for hours from sun-up to sun-down. Parents never worried about their whereabouts or what their kids were up-to. Playing and having fun occupied a kid's mind. No one was ever board. By bed time when the sun was setting a kid would be plum tuckered out. Shut-eye would happen when their heads hit the softness of the pillow. Dreams were dreamt about the next day's activities.

Behind Johnson's house Francis and his bunch were congregating near the tall grass. The boys were resting leaning against two fifteen-foot poles with a header across the top. Francis was showing the other boys how to tie a hangman's noose on the rope he had. Everyone was paying close attention.

Then with a surprise the north end cowboys crossed the street and took the other boys by surprise. Shots were fired as voices called out. "I got you." They had no chance and quickly surrendered.

"Plan on having a hanging?" asked Jerry as he eyed the rope with a half-made loop.

Francis drawled. "If we ever find a bad guy."

With wide-eyed intrigue the younger boys glanced at each other and the rope that was taking on a menacing shape.

"We know how to hang a bad guy. . .." Tom's eyes grew tight with the lids becoming slits. ". . . Just like they do in the movies."

Mark stepped closer with a bit of cockiness he asked. "How do you plan on doing that?"

"When we find a bad guy or a volunteer." Francis left the statement open for a moment. "Then we will show you how it is done."

"There ain't no bad guys here is there Pat?" Richard whispered as Pat shrugged his shoulders.

"Do you know what volunteer means?" asked Pat of Richard.

Pat gave a questioning look towards his brother Tom. Pat was not so sure that his blonde haired blue-eyed brother was telling the truth.

Francis stood displaying the round loop with laps of rope circling the main rope that would slip and tighten the noose. Was it a real scene from an old time western? Some cowboys sat against the poles, others stood leaning on their play rifles. All kept a questioning eye on the rope.

Terry was not afraid of his brother Francis. "Then show us how it works."

Francis turned and gave the rope a toss towards the header crossing near the top of the poles. "I will. I still need a volunteer."

Even without knowing the meaning of the word the younger boys moved a step back to be on the cautious side. Tom squinted at the boys. It was hard to think of Tom as a mean kid, after-all Tom was an altar boy. Here and now Tom was holding his knowledge over the rest.

"They do not really hang people in the movies." bragged Tom.

Pat, Billy and Mark quickly replied in order to show that they were not dummies. "We know that."

Tom looked towards the top of the poles. "When Francis gets the rope over the cross-bar I will show you."

For the third try Francis tossed the brown woven hemp rope towards the cross bar. Each time it came closer but without success.

After thinking for a while, Jerry came to the conclusion that there had to be a trick to this hanging. "You need two ropes, one they tie around under your arms."

"You do not see two ropes in the movies." puffed Francis as he struggled with the uncooperative rope.

Suddenly from out of the tall grass came several boys that startled the Roosevelt Street cowboys. Surely, they had to be the bad guys.

"What are you up to Francis?" asked one of the boys. "We just came over to see what you guys' were doing."

"We were playing cowboys." replied Terry with confidence that he hoped he knew what he was doing. "You guy's interested in playing?"

"You guys can be the bad guys." Surely Tom knew what point Terry was getting to.

"We need bad guys to capture then Francis is going to show us how they hang bad guys in the movies."

"You guys do not know how to do that." said one of the new strangers. Several of the other boys shook their heads side to side.

Francis held the rope out to show them it's quality. Each boy in turn inspected the handiwork. "If I had a longer rope, I would show you. This one is not long enough to toss over the crossbar."

All eyes looked skyward. A weathered two-by-six looked dark grey against the darkening clouds of late afternoon. In the stillness of the moment before a coming storm Mother's voices began to sound through the neighborhood.

"Time for supper." Billy's Mother called out.

"Pat . . . Tom."

"Jerry, supper time . . ., tell Richard, Bart and Mark that it is time for them to go home for supper too.

"Terry . . . Francis."

From across the field the Mothers of the new boys were calling out their respective names.

"We have to go." one boy said, his dark brown eyes still held the question of how could Francis hang someone like they do in the movies. "You guys' going to play cowboys after supper?"

"Sure are." Tom and Francis assured them.

"You guys will have to be the bad guys." added Terry.

"Okay."

With the wind blowing across the tall brown grass, the boys of the street headed home for supper. In their minds was the anticipation of having a good gun fight now that there would be bad guys.

Richard quickly downed his supper without a word of how the day had gone or of what his new hurry was. His brown leather double holster was still strapped to his hips. Between mouthfuls Richard's eyes glanced out of the kitchen window. Beyond the yellow curtains the sky seemed darker as the clouds seemed to be climbing over each other.

Before Mom was able to stop him, Richard bolted out of the door, crossed yards and ditches to come to a stop in Johnson's back yard. There he stood staring at the two poles with a header high above him. None of the other boys were there yet. Richard waited until the rain from the heavens began to fall.

Nothing ever happened after that day. Sure, the Roosevelt Street boys still played cowboys. The guys from the next street over came by to play, and they were the bad guys. Tom and Francis never mentioned the hanging trick. The rope was never seen again.

REMEMBERING
CHAPTER 4
SKATING RINK

"May I go now?" asked Richard as he gazed out of the frosted pains of glass. "I can see the rink."

Winter came and stayed on Roosevelt Street. Houses were hidden from the street by snow banks that seemed twenty feet tall. At lest that is what it seemed like to a five-year-old. Cutting across the back yards to visit friends was a matter of spending hours ploughing through the waist-deep snow.

This winter after the Pelletiers moved in, Mr. Pelletier made an ice rink for his children. Water steamed from the water hose and instant ice formed when the water hit the packed snow. Mark and Richard helped pack the snow down with small snowshoes. Mr. Pelletier rolled the snow with a big round roller filled with water.

For Mr. Pelletier the making of a rink was hard work. Mark and Richard did not think so, to them it was an adventure in progress. Early morning and late at night Mr. Pelletier bundled up in layers of clothes fought off the cold of a Northern Ontario winter. The rink needed to be watered.

Getting ready to go skating was a ritual. If Richard was going through it no doubt Mark was having the same plight. Richard stood and sat on command at the stairs leading to the back door. At each command that Mom made Teddy the dog responded. Teddy did not have to wear exactly the same amount of clothes as Richard did. Most of the time Teddy ran around naked just like one of the girls that lived on the south side of the Mousseau's house. Just in the summer time did the girl do this.

Sit then stand, lift right leg, lift left leg, both arms. This was an early version of aerobics. Under layer upon layer of clothes was a skinny kid with enough padding to play in the big league of Canadian hockey.

Finally, the skates were tied, Richard was ready. A cloud of cold steam formed when warm house air met the cold of winter. The outside door was open. Teddy retreated to the comfort of warm air rising from the heating duct. With insulated attire, Richard did not feel the cold blast of winter's air. Mom wrapped her house coat tighter around herself as she opened the outside door in front of her little son.

"I am on my wa . . .," mumbled words were all that came from Richard's lips. Mom pulled a big flannel scarf around his nose and mouth. Only specks of brown eyes peered out of the Rolly-Polly boy.

A gentle hand guided him out into the cold of a winter wonderland. The clink, clink of skate blades on the entrance gave way to the squeak, squeak of warm steel on hard packed snow.

"Have fun Richard." inspired Mom. Through the door's curtains Mom watched Richard waddle towards the ice rink, towards Mark waddling his way out of his home.

Squeak, squeak . . ., squeak, squeak. Alternating echoes of squeaks filled the morning air. Mark and Richard made their way towards each other. Round dark dots behind woven cloth stared at each other.

'Who is that strange bundle.' thought Richard. 'He came out of Mark's house.'

Stopping a foot apart Richard and Mark eyed each other up and down without saying a word. As if looking at their own reflection in a mirror. Toques, scarfs, coats, heavy pants and mitts. Only slight differences in colour. The brown eyes staring out of the bundles at each other was truly an eerie sensation.

"Hi Richard." came Mark's muffled greeting.

"Hi." Richard reciprocated in an equally muffled voice.

Off they headed through the knee-deep snow towards the beckoning ice-skating rink. Puffs of hot breath through the scarves cooled and created tiny icicles that hung from coloured fibers. Just ahead shimmered the clear blue ice in the morning light. Not a scrape or gouge. Smooth and hard. Looking down onto the ice their slightly distorted images reflected back to the hesitating boys.

There they stood at the edge of the frozen body of water. Shiny chrome plated ice blades sparkled. Mark's dad had sharpened the blades to glide freely over the ice. One step and off they would go with the exhilaration of floating effortlessly like seasoned hockey players.

On the sidelines, they stood each waiting for the other to take the first step. Mark made the first move, his skate tested the ice that curved up to meet the snow bank. Right behind Mark, Richard stepped with one foot onto the ice.

It was the exhilaration of overcoming nature. Their brown eyes widened with pride. From each other to the ice then to the heavens their eyes encompassed the spectrum. Plump padded bodies headed head over heels to land flat on their backs.

Amazing is the fact that things happened so quickly. In the matter of a second, aspirations became deflated efforts. At such a young age, do all children look upon their daily experiences as a blue print of what their future lives would entail? Was this first attempt at ice skating, the reality of all things to come?

Two small children rocked and rolled fighting against the bulk of layered clothes. After what seemed prolonged minutes, Mark and Richard sat up gazing in bewilderment at each other. Mark pushed back his sagging toque that covered his eyes. After pulling down a plaid scarf Richard gulped in a breath of cold air.

Doing the same Mark said matter of fact. "This ice is pretty hard."

With a mitt, Richard patted the ice and nodded in agreement.

"My dad made a pretty good rink." Mark nodded his head, his hand began buffing up a patch of ice.

What seemed like hours these two best friends discussed the meaning of life, this was according to a child's perspective. Every inch of that ice rink was covered and explored on hands and knees, stomachs, backs and butts. Not once did an ice skate carve a grove into the splendid ice surface that Mark's dad made.

Today years after his childhood does Mark tell his children of what it was like to live in Northern Ontario as a child in the late fifties? Richard lost track of Mark's whereabouts after high-school. To meet each other now would it be like the past. Maybe Richard would jot a few stories down to rekindle old memories.

Every chance Richard happened to have, back during the cold winter of the late fifties, he would lace up those skates. Mom would do the actual tightening of the laces. All bundled up he would make his way to Mark's rink. Step by step, slide, teeter and regain his balance then continue his practice.

Some times skating with Mark and sometimes alone until the day came to an end. Through those long cold winter days Richard and Mark mastered the art of skating. Mark and Richard had conquered the frozen ice in the back yard of Mark's house on Roosevelt Street.

THINGS THAT HAPPEN
CHAPTER 5
SCARLET FEVER

Spring was on its way out but fall had not quite arrived to the north. Just the day before Billy, Bart, Richard and Mark had been making the rounds. Each yard had to be explored, that included ditches, hedges, puddles and fields. Boys were being boys playing and enjoying the youth of being young.

Never were they destructive or mean. What they did with their time was to explore and be amazed by what nature had to offer. In the early months of fall there was not much of the nature to see. Birds had now flown south; spiders and frogs were burrowing into the hardening mud of the earth.

Dark clouds filled with oncoming winter snow flakes passed overhead. Cool winds tried to penetrate hats and the summer coats as the boys explored another field. While Bart, Billy and Mark eagerly moved from one interest to another, Richard lagged behind. Nature was interesting, but on this day the energy Richard should have had, was not there.

"Richard, hurry up!" yelled Mark as he and the others jumped a ditch and disappeared into a field behind Billy's house.

"Okay . . . I am coming." said Richard as he stood still until he lost sight of the boys.

Above the sky seemed to move in slow motion. Richard's feet moved just as slow on the gravel road. Unaware of his surroundings his eyes watched his feet take a step then another.

"Hi Richard . . ., what are you doing?" said a girl's voice. Laura, the girl next door, began walking beside him. "Where are you going?"

Laura was about a year older and a little bit more aggressive and adventurous. Maybe the shy Richard liked that about this skinny blonde haired girl. Though he might have had feelings towards her, he never spoke words containing his thoughts. For as long as they resided on Roosevelt Street Richard never ever mentioned his feelings towards her.

"Are you going home?" Laura put her arm on Richard's shoulder and walked a few steps until another interest grabbed her thoughts and attention. "See you later Richard."

Richard continued on towards home while the events of the day lingered abstractly in his thoughts. Mom was at the kitchen counter doing some baking. Music played softly on the radio as he entered the back door and removed his shoes and coat. Teddy lifted his head questionably as Richard walked past on his way to the big red-flowered couch. Mom noticed but paid no important interest in his early arrival home.

That big red couch with huge arms was pretending horses, horses of imagination for Richard and younger brother Donald. Today there would be no saddling up and riding. With a click of the television knob the black and white set hummed while a picture focused into view. Huddling into the corner of the couch where security surrounded him and kept at-bay the images coming from the television.

Randolph Scott rode across the screen on a horse with his six-shooter firing at pursuing bad guys. In nineteen-fifty-nine a cowboy's hero came to life on the little black and white screen. Cowboy folklore filled the imagination of Richard's mind.

Sleep came and lingered, time passed. With blurry eyes Richard looked up from his bed. Mom was with a man she called Doctor. She placed a cool towel on the fevered child's forehead while the doctor lifted one eyelid then the other. A cold round shinny thing, with a tube that went to the doctor's ears, was placed on Richard's beat red chest. All the words spoken were mumbled, he could not make sense of the strange words. At six years of age all that medical talking did not mean much to a sick child.

What registered in Richard's mind was the name of his affliction. 'Scarlet Fever . . . Scarlet Fever!' His eyes closed, sleep came and lingered.

☐☐☐☐

Dreams linger when one is asleep, as if still pictures were moving in random order. In Richard's sub-conscience, these pictures flowed vividly, showing the events of the past summer.

Hot and lingering weather. It seemed as if everyone was outside. From morning to late night neighbors mingled. Kids flowed freely. If strangers had visited, they would not know whose children belonged to whom. In everyone's back yard something was happening. People migrated to one home, then after a period of time, they would drift to the next backyard.

This one day the boys of all ages were hanging around the McAuley's back yard. Mr. McAuley was out in the back yard taking care of his chickens. He was in the process of taking care of them for good.

Two doors south at the Sullivan's home some girls were gathered playing girl's games. It seemed that at that time in life there was a distinction between what boys did and what was expected from girls. Sharon and Laura were about the same age. Both skinny looking, blondes and somewhat like tom boys.

Each girl of all ages took their turn at the hopscotch game carved into the gravel driveway. Sharon had on floppy sandal shoes that clopped every time she tried to hop, skip and jump. A skimpy yellow nylon summer dress stuck to her body from the summer heat. With the day lingering long everyone was feeling the effects of the sun's rays beating down.

□□□□

Chunk! came the sound of a hatchet axe against the hardwood block of wood. Another headless chicken flopped around the ground at Mr. McAuley's feet. Tom, Pat, Terry, Richard, Jerry, Billy and Mark were gathered around watching the nature of life take its course.

People eat chicken and love to eat chicken. In order to have the pleasure of a good meal someone has to raise and slaughter the chicken. For the boys, hanging around the chopping block, this event seemed natural.

Tom scurried around the chicken pen trying to grab hold of a plump chicken. Feathers flew as the chased chicken baulked. Other birds knowing of their impending doom scattered to the far corners of the pen.

Tom's quick hand handed a caught chicken to his father. One fatal swish and another headless chicken headed nowhere fast. It was up to all of the boys gathered to pick up a chicken and wait in line.

Toys were toys. But the magic of a chicken foot that moved, now that was something. Each young boy had to have one. Mr. McAuley relished in the notion that he was able to show the boys how to make a chicken's foot move.

One by one a boy handed his chicken to Mr. McAuley who in turn loped off a chicken leg just above the knee. With a slice from his pocket knife a portion of the scaly skin was peeled back. Motioning to each boy to bend down close Mr. McAuley pulled on the white tendon near the leg bone. Each and every boy jumped back as the claws of the chicken leg sprang open in their face.

Billy was the last in line with his chicken. Billy was sort of short and chubby for his age. But he was the best street hockey goalie around, a real Gump Worsley. That was a winter story, this was summer. As luck would have it something was wrong with Billy's chicken foot. Each time Mr. McAuley pulled on the chicken's tendon only the middle toe would spring up. Having an odd ball chicken foot was kind of cool and different than the other fellow's chicken's feet. 'This foot would scare the girls the best.' thought Billy.

With their magic chicken feet in hand the boys went off to play. Left behind were the few live chickens in the chicken pen with terrified eyes. Mr. McAuley hunched over to begin plucking another chicken.

   □□□□

Summer's days were warm and sunny with pleasant cool nights. Cool evenings when people wanted to stay out of doors and socialize. Some leaned back in lawn chairs and studied the milky way. Anticipating an evening like this Mr. Sullivan started a small backyard bon-fire. Dry wood, old logs, tree branches he gathered in a pile and started his fire.

The boys came by to scare the girls with their chicken claws then departed to find other unsuspecting victims. Sharon and Laura shrugged off the chicken foot attack and carried on with their game of hop-scotch.

When the play drifted towards skip-rope Laura's eyes caught sight of Mrs. Birch across the street.

"Sharon." Laura tugged on Sharon's dress. "Mrs. Birch is watering her flowers."

"I see." answered an unimpressed Sharon.

"Do you want to go cool off under the water?" Laura pushed her blonde hair away from her face and the stickiness of play on her cheeks.

Before Sharon could answer Laura was already heading to her home. It did not take long for Laura to shed her clothes in the driveway then head across the street buck naked. Her little green shorts were discarded by the corner of the house, a yellow top left on the steps, shoes and underpants left in a pile near the front of her house. A clean exit from her yard to the gravel road to the Birch's yard.

"Spray me." called out the naked little girl to Mrs. Birch. "Spray me."

Turning with the water hose in hand Mrs. Birch watched a blur of a blonde-haired fair skinned naked little girl jumping up and down with glee.

"Spray me!"

"Laura! What are you doing without clothes on?" Mrs. Birch smiled at this child's spontaneous actions.

"It is hot out. I want to swim under the water." Laura motioned with her hands for Mrs. Birch to spray her.

"Did your mother say it was okay?"

Laura returned an innocent white lie. "Yes . . . it is okay."

Before Mrs. Birch, was able to question further, Laura's younger sister Valerie was disrobing on the front lawn. Realizing that the day was hot it would be of no harm to cool down the children under the water hose.

Where there is fun to be had, children will congregate. Soon other girls joined in, though not as naked as Laura and Valerie. Mrs. Birch handed the hose to the children to play with to their content. With glee, she watched childhood innocence with her own reminiscence of being young.

In other backyards, the boys chased each other and unsuspecting victims with their chicken claws. Late afternoon brought a laziness to the neighborhood. Mothers began the evening meal, fathers slowly ceased their chores to lounge under a small shade tree. Children never seem to slow down. After standing still for a moment or so; they are off at full speed into another adventure.

"Put your clothes back on!" yelled Mrs. Thibodeau from out of her kitchen window. "That is enough water for today. Get dressed."

Reluctantly and with much hesitation Laura and Valerie managed to get half dressed.

"What happened?" asked Laura of a boy that came by with a chicken foot.

Mrs. Thibodeau leaned towards the open window. No sooner had the words left his lips then word of the news was passed from neighbor to neighbor. Mrs. Thibodeau, Mrs. Mousseau and Mrs. McAuley dropped their preparations of an evening meal to hurry to the Sullivan's backyard. Richard watched his mom fly by the McAuley's backyard as she jumped a small ditch and disappear behind balsam trees.

Being kids means trying out things for themselves, learning from experience. No doubt younger children watch and emulate older children. Thus the events of the day. Around and around and over Mr. Sullivan's bon-fire the older girls leaped. Oh the excitement and adrenalin rush of success.

Logs on the fire were now glowing coals with hardly any flames. Sharon leaped after a hesitated start. Before a blink of an eye a yellow flowered nylon dress shriveled onto Sharon's side. Her leap fell short. After falling onto her side on to the hot coals she rolled off onto the cool ground.

Screams filled the afternoon stillness. Men awoke from siestas, mothers ran towards a child's scream. Word spread like wild-fire. Everyone came to the rescue. A yellow flowered dress melted onto Sharon's skin. Tears flowed freely down her cheeks, shivers of fear shook Sharon's body. A game of adventure turned to an experience of life's lessons.

Quickly one mother applied wet towels to the girl's side and upper hip. A car's engine roared to life as a mother and child enter the back seat. Dust billowed behind the automobile as it sped towards the city hospital. Thoughts and stories flowed from mouth to ears as dust settled onto the gravel road.

"She will be just fine." assured Mrs. McAuley.

"Yes, yes." replied Mrs. Thibodeau. "You children stay away from that fire." She took Valerie's hand. "Laura, get dressed. Put your top on."

Sharon was going to be just fine. Scars at childhood would fade as she grew older. After several years, the Sullivans moved. Surely Sharon grew up to be a beautiful person with a slight flaw from a childhood adventure.

󠀠󠀠󠀠󠀠 ▢▢▢▢

Weeks seemed to pass in the month of September before Richard's sleep was awakened. The changing of the fall season was missed, the colours of the rainbow falling in different leaf shapes. Crab apples and red apples had fallen to the ground to be devoured by worms. A life time of child's play was missed. A part of Richard's life had passed him by. Even though it was only several weeks it was several weeks of time Richard would not be able to get back. A child does not want to miss any amount of time.

Weak from fever, blistered and peeling from his aliment, Richard slowly moved about. Life seemed new, everything held a new fascination. Mark was outside wondering why his best Pal could not come out to play. 'Soon.' Mark was told by Richard's Mom.

Dreams of the past summer's adventures in the neighborhood flowed like a movie in Richard's mind during those days that he had slept. Yes, dreams kept him in touch with life and with the neighborhood.

The chicken foot did not work anymore. Richard left it on the dresser as a souvenir. Without a great amount of speed, though he wanted to hurry, Richard dressed for his first day outside playing with his pal Mark. Roosevelt Street looked different but stayed the same.

THINGS THAT HAPPEN
CHAPTER 6
DOGS AND CATS

They come and go those dogs and cats. They achieve no great fame. They lay forgotten in unmarked graves. It seems funny that dogs and cats live such short lives. As people, we cherish our memories as if pets had lived in our lives forever. Where are all those forgotten grave sites of our pets so many years ago?

Bart lived at the head of the street. He was quiet, different than his older brother. Bart grew slowly, he was on the short side until he had made a growth spurt in his high-school years. As a young kid with soft features and thin brown hair it seemed that at times that he faded into the background of a crowd. At times, it seemed that he was there but not there.

The first time that Mark and Richard went to play at Bart's house it was the view of the front steps that caught their eyes. They had seen the same scene in pictures on television showing black and white images from Egypt. Both Mark and Richard looked inquisitively at each other with the same strange thoughts in their minds.

"Look at that." both said simultaneously.

Bart's house faced the creek. The back of the house faced Roosevelt Street. A big section of frosted blocks of glass was framed by red brick on the back porch. Cement steps protruded from the enclosed porch alongside of the house wall. A patio walk lead to the driveway and to the road where Mark and Richard stood staring at the house.

On the cement landing of the steps, sitting at each end, sitting tall and still were two Siamese cats. Like statutes guarding the Queen's palace. Both boys ease slowly towards the steps. There was no movement from the tall thin cats. Not an eye twitched on the golden coloured felines.

"Are they real?" Mark asked of Richard.

"They look real."

"Do they bite?"

"No . . ., I do not think so." answered Richard as he placed chilled hands into his pockets.

Mysteries of life affect even boys of seven years old. Questions and answers arrive in life at any moment. At a moment in life what one does, affects how they will deal with life in the future. To take a chance and forge ahead early in life will eliminate some of the fear in later life. Some children hide and let life unfold before they are able to feel safe that life will not hurt them. Some take a chance, though it is such a small insignificant moment in life.

"You go first." motioned Mark for Richard to walk along the patio slabs.

"Me . . ., Bart is your friend first." Richard shoved his hands deeper into his corduroy pant's pockets.

Mark's hands were already stuffed deep into the pockets of his coat. He shrugged his shoulders burying his neck deep into the coat's collar. "Just at school he is my first friend. You do not like cats?"

"Naw . . ., but I ain't scared of them." Richard took several sliding steps along the patio slabs. "Those are pretty big cats eh Mark?"

"Yeah!" agreed Mark with a slightly raised pitch in his voice.

They just sat there those two Siamese cats. Sitting and staring without moving. Curled tails were rapped around their paws. Eyes of green emeralds with vertical slits were frozen in a stare. They were staring at two small boys trying to visit their friend Bart.

It only took five minutes for Richard and Mark to walk from down the street to Bart's house. Maybe fifteen minutes had passed from the time the boy's eyes caught sight of those cats sitting menacing looking on the back porch. Fifteen minutes to walk from the driveway to the first porch step.

"Do not look at the cats directly in the eyes." Mark called out from his position at the corner of the house.

Richard was inching his way towards the steps, up the steps' one at a time towards the door that seemed out of reach. From the door to the side of the house to the street his eyes gazed at everything except the piercing eyes of the Siamese cats.

With a quick rap of his little knuckles on the door the echo of his knock sounded like a boom. With lightning speed Richard returned his hand to the safety of his pocket. No answer came to the door. Looking towards Mark, Richard saw the heads of the cats move in the bottom of his own brown eyes. Those cats were ready to pounce.

Mark pointed towards the door with a bobbing motion of his head. "Knock again . . . this time louder."

"No one is home." replied Richard as he knocked again. This time the knock seemed to boom even louder.

Pleasantly Mrs. Bradley opened the inside door then the screen door. "Hello."

"Is Bart home?" asked Richard without hesitation.

"Yes, he is . . ., come in . . ., Mark, you too." invited Mrs. Bradley.

Mark rushed to the door keeping his body close to the side of the house. With a slight sigh of relief, the boys stood inside of the porch. Behind them Mrs. Bradley closed the door leaving the cat creatures in the outside world.

Forgotten are life's inconveniences when children are at play. That is until play is over and it is time to go home. Getting dressed in the porch surely made Richard and Mark wondered if those cats were still outside guarding the Queen's palace. Once the door was open and if the cats were still there the boys would make a quick getaway.

Bart pulled hard on the solid wood door. "See you at school tomorrow."

"Okay." answered the departing guests.

There they were, two Siamese cats staring with hunger in their big wide eyes. Hands were safely stuffed into pockets. With their backs to the cats the two scurried down the steps, along the patio slabs to the driveway. Not until they were halfway along the driveway did the boy's turn to wave their goodbyes.

"Bye, Bart."

No one was there to receive the boy's goodbye. The door was closed and Bart was gone. Two golden coloured Siamese cats, sitting like stone carved statutes, peered at two boys standing at a safe distance on the gravel bed on Roosevelt Street.

☐☐☐☐

Teddy was a dog, not a special dog with breading or having special papers. Teddy was just a dog that needed a place to lay his head and have good meals offered to him. Uncle Ray, Dad's younger brother brought a dog home for Richard when he was four going on five years of age. How old the dog was no one knew? Uncle Ray found the dog when he was working in the bush. When Uncle Ray was making supper for himself, back in the bush far from town this hungry dog came sniffing around. The dog looked like a mixed terrier. As dad would explain, he was a Heinz-fifty-seven. Richard figured a Heinz-fifty-seven was the type of breed. To his friends, that was how he introduced his new dog.

After days of tossing scraps of food and talking kind words to the stray dog Uncle Ray began a friendship. When his bush work was completed and the trucks were loaded to leave Uncle Ray peered into the eyes of the lonely looking dog. A short-whistled invitation was the deciding point for the dog. Somehow the dog knew that going was much better than staying.

Now a dog needs a place to live. Uncle Ray worked and was single at the time. So, he kind-of dropped the dog off at his brother Fern's place. 'It was a gift for Richard.' Uncle Ray had said. That was that, Fern could not refuse a gift.

Teddy became the Dog's name at his new residence. Food, a warm place to live and a playmate came with the deal. For Teddy, the terms were agreeable and enjoyable. Richard and Teddy hit it off quite well. Animals have a sense of knowing that children will not hurt them. Teddy held out a cautious eye for older children and adults. It is a study of nature to observe the temperament of a dog when being prodded, pulled and hugged by children. Without a bark or bite Teddy accepted the rough loving from Richard and friends.

'Stray dog is adopted by Richard and given a new home.' quoted the headline over the picture of Teddy and Richard in the local Sault Star newspaper. A young boy hugging his new dog and offering him a cookie was their minute of fame. It is unfortunate that dogs age faster than their human counter part. As Richard grew older and more alive with adventure Teddy aged and spent more time sleeping on the warm gravel of the drive.

No matter how sound asleep he was, if a stranger happened by or someone pulled into the driveway Teddy was up and ready to inspect the situation. Dogs seem to accept their security role. Along with the role of babysitter, pillow and squeeze-toy.

Jerry, who lived next door, came over one day to play, Teddy snapped and growled at him. Richard and Jerry were good friends though Jerry was a couple of years older. On this day, Teddy must have sensed something odd. It was the first time and only time that Teddy had ever reacted that way.

The next day Jerry stood at the property line near the broken-down fence waiting for Richard to come outside to play. Jerry hesitated when Richard invited him over to play.

"It is okay . . . my dog likes you." said Richard as he patted Teddy on the top of the head. Sad forgiving eyes peered up from the black and white-haired dog.

"He does not like me . . . he will bite me." Jerry slowly edged his way towards Richard and Teddy. It took Jerry awhile but he managed to stroke the top of Teddy's head. Teddy's eyes rolled with pleasure from the soft pat. Now they were friends and yesterday's incident was all but forgotten.

So, it went on for several years that kids were kids and Teddy was Teddy. Though Teddy managed to wander off more often to rest and soak up the warmth of the sun.

When Richard was seven, growing as fast as a bad weed, life's unpredictability happened. Jerry and Richard were busy playing in the back yard while Teddy assumed his sleeping position in the front driveway. An accumulation of events happened randomly with no logical reason.

Two houses north lived the Scotts. They had two girls, one Richard's age and one four years younger about the age of Richard's brother Donald. Mrs. Scott, was about the only mother on the street, that drove an automobile.

Was she in a hurry or absent minded this day when she left her home and headed south on Roosevelt Street? Mrs. Scott was down near the Birch's house when she remembered that she had forgotten something at home. Putting her car in reverse, she began to back up towards her house. Why did she not drive backwards all the way home, what changed her mind to decide to back up into the Mousseau's driveway?

Hearing a stranger's car sputter Teddy awoke from his dreams. Age, or a slowing reaction from Teddy, or the speed of the car, were unknown facts. There was no time to change the pending outcome.

"What was that?" questioned Mrs. Scott to herself.

A sudden bump rocked the rear end of her car. Teddy limped away from his resting spot. The pain from the car's tire running over the dog's hip made Teddy yelp in anguish.

Everyone's ears perked, Mom, Richard and Jerry heard the yelping of an injured animal. The cry of pain sent shivers up the spins of everyone in hearing range. Mrs. Scott was now out on the street before she realized what had happened.

With ears limp, eyes wet and a whimper each time he made a step Teddy dragged his crushed body past Richard's shocked eyes. Helplessly Richard held out comforting arms. Teddy sighed limping away towards the house door held open by Mom. Down to the cool basement Teddy went to lay down his crumpled body.

It was about the first time that Richard heard, and was able to understand life through the lyrics of a song. On the radio, Elvis sang the heart wrenching lyrics of a tale of a boy and his dog. Etched in Richard's mind was the happy and tragic life of Ole Shep.

Days passed and each day Richard would stand at the top of the basement stairs calling down to Teddy to come up for food. Down into the darkened basement Richard would go to visit his pal. Teddy laid there with weakened heart his will to satisfy hunger gone. A will to struggle to live was fading. Wanting eyes questioned his state. Comforting hands stroked the soft black hair above Teddy's tear filled eyes. Richard could feel the shallow weak breath, the cool air from Teddy's open mouth. Both boy and dog peered deep into each other's eyes. Were their thoughts and feelings able to comfort each other?

Nothing was explained when Uncle Ray carried a whimpering Teddy up the stairs and laid him gently in the back seat of his car, the car that brought Teddy to Richard.

"It is time for Teddy to go to a better place." Mom said to Richard as the house door closed behind a departing Teddy. Her words were soft, Richard taking comfort in the thought that Teddy would be in a better place.

Richard often recalls the words to the song 'Old Shep' and wonders if Uncle Ray was able to carry out his undeserving responsibilities.

"With hands that were trembling I picked up my gun and aimed it at Shep's faithful head."

"Now old Shep he is gone where the good doggies go and no more with old Shep will I roam."

"If dog's have a heaven there is one thing I know, old Shep has a wonderful home." sang Elvis from the radio.

A held back tear is in Richard's eye each time he sings that song so many years after Teddy left Roosevelt Street.

□□□□

Winter arrived in a flurry of snow and below normal temperatures. From early November, the temperature fell below thirty degrees Fahrenheit and stayed there until the sun of late March managed to penetrate dark clouds. Snow piled high as high as an eight-year-old standing on his pal's shoulders.

Mark and Richard were up early and bundled up ready to venture out into the wonderland of a Northern Ontario winter. Street hockey was great this year. Plenty of hard packed snow on the road to give a good hockey surface. No salt or sand was put on side roads in the nineteen-sixties so that made conditions ideal for all-day play. With rubber boots you could slip and slide, shoot and score while sliding spread eagle and taking out six other kids that were in your way.

Billy Wozny, short and chubby, was a real great imitation of Gump Worsley, the famous hockey goalie. Mark and Richard headed down the street towards Billy's home. Hockey was the objective and Billy was going to be asked to play. As usual the long way had to be taken, each driveway, each tall snowbank had to be explored, climbed and rolled down. Cold, hell it was cold but not cold enough to stop two kids from enjoying winter.

In Northern Ontario where winter came and stayed, where people dressed to ward off the cold and the houses constantly puffed heat of grey smoke into the sky, how did those people survive? Gone were the birds of summer. Worms and moles were bedded down deep below the earth. Squirrels and chipmunks were sleeping the winter away nestled in their dens.

"Do creek fish hibernate?" asked Richard as he slid down another snow bank.

Mark pondered the question during his belly slide towards the road. "I think they get frozen in the water . . . then in the summer after the ice melts they swim away."

Seven-year-old kids have the questions and answers to life's mysteries. If only life's question could be answered so simply.

"They just come back alive?" another question Richard asked during his slide down the snow bank.

Right behind him Mark bumped into Richard sending both of them onto the road. "Yup." was all that Mark replied.

Picking up their hockey sticks both boys began passing a blue and red white striped ball along the road. Richard wanted to be Rocket Richard a Montreal Canadian hockey great but Mark claimed him first. Richard ended up being the Pocket Richard a brother of the Rocket. Both were Montreal Canadians so the names were okay.

"How come there is nobody else out playing hockey?" asked Mark. With the back of his leather mitt he wiped the cold-water droplet from his nose.

"I do not know. It is a great day to play hockey." informed Richard shrugging his shoulders. Mark agreed by mimicking with the same body language.

Sure, it was a great day for street hockey. The snow plough had passed, the road was slippery, then why? Most people are late risers in winter. Mark and Richard were early risers but maybe too early. Most people were turning over in bed seeking that extra half hour of sleep on a Saturday morning. Eight o'clock on a Saturday morning is not too early.

Billy's house was still asleep. There were no house lights on, no window curtains open. Standing at the end of the driveway looking at the slate house in an off colour blue the boys questioned themselves.

"Do you think Billy is up yet?"

"I think so Mark . . . maybe not."

"Let's go see." demanded Mark, thinking that if he and Richard were up so should Billy.

Climbing over the snowdrift at the driveway's end Mark and Richard, made deep footprints in the fresh snow of last night's snowfall. The clear morning brought the temperature down a few more degrees.

"It is cold enough to freeze pee." Mark quoted with authority.

"I am going to wait until I get home." Richard assured himself.

Rounding the back corner of the house Mark and Richard stopped in mid-step. Eyes and thoughts focused on an old tire and rim sitting just under the front end of a blocked-up car. Billy's little short haired dog lay on its side with little legs stretched out stiffly, lifeless as if it was a plastic toy dog.

"Is it dead?" Mark wiped his nose on the back of his ice-covered mitt. His face scrunched up from the scratching pain of flesh against ice.

"I think so. It is not breathing." Leaning over using his hockey stick for support, Richard took a closer look. "It is not breathing Mark."

"It must have died last night." Mark leaned closer. "It was real cold last night. Billy's dog did not have enough hair on it to keep warm."

"Nothing to keep it warm." Richard lifted the blade of his hockey stick and touched the dog's back end. "The dog is hard just like frozen ice."

Mark poked the dog softly with his hockey stick. "I wonder if Billy knows that his dog is dead."

"I do not think anyone is up yet. Billy must have forgot about bringing the dog into the house last night."

Hovering over the still cold body of the dog Mark and Richard contemplated on what the right procedure was they should take. After all they found the dog in its present state.

"I think we should go." Richard brought up a new line of thought. "They might think we killed it."

"No . . ., the dog froze to death." confirmed Mark, he looked around the near vicinity. "Maybe we should bury the dog so that Billy does not see it."

"Yeah, it might hurt his feelings, he might start to cry." said Richard, keeping his eyes on the still body. He silently hoped that the dog would wake up. Recalled memories of Teddy gave Richard a clear understanding of how Billy would feel. "I think we should bury the dog then tell Billy's Mom."

"The snow is too deep to reach the ground."

"Mark, we have no shovel and the ground will be too hard to dig into."

Leaning on their hockey sticks they held a silent thought for the passing of a family pet to the after life where it was warm.

"Let's bury him under the snow." suggested Mark, his nose dripping from the cold.

"Okay."

With their sticks, they scooped the snow up and gently covered the tiny dog. Surely it would only be temporary. Mr. Wozny would bury it later in the spring. After their good deed was accomplished the boys turned towards the back door of the house. Removing his ice-covered mitt Mark knocked on the aluminum door. After a second and a third knock Mrs. Wozny opened the door. Respectful eyes stared at the curlers wrapped in a hair net on Mrs. Wozny's head.

"Good morning Mark and Richard." greeted Mrs. Wozny. "Billy is not out of bed yet."

"That is okay." assured Mark quickly. "We had to bury Billy's dog."

"Over there." pointed Richard to the mound of fresh snow. "It froze last night. It was cold, real cold.

"We did not want Billy to see his dog dead." Mark turned his eyes away from Mrs. Wozny.

"Oh....thank you." Mrs. Wozny looked towards the mound of snow. There was sad concern in her disappointed voice. "That was nice of you to bury Billy's dog. I will tell him later."

"Tell Billy we will see him later." requested Mark, he tried to put on a brave face. "Maybe tomorrow."

Mark and his pal Richard slowly retraced their footsteps down the driveway to the street. Maybe Billy would be okay tomorrow or the next day. Street hockey on Roosevelt Street needed a good goalie.

FIELDS TO EXPLORE
CHAPTER 7
ROCK SALT

Before the second world war there was a time of excitement and relaxation. Not everyone was afforded the ability to indulge in relaxation, but a few were.

Two-streets west of Roosevelt Street is Brookfield Street. A field is there where after the war a school was built. St. Francis School occupied a little section of the south end of the field. Looking from the north to the south, the field stretched for a mile. Tall elm trees stood like guards at the north end. Patches of bushes lined the south-west end near a creek that ran through the centre of the field. Across the creek, the field was just as wide and long. A great place for the kids of Roosevelt Street to explore.

Few people residing in the new subdivisions surrounding the field remembered, or even knew of the golf course that once graced the ragged field. Little was left after world war two. A club house near the creek, several old pole barns and patches of dark green grass was all that was left to see.

But before, in a time when men dressed in knickers and white golf shoes, the field was organized. Light green grass mowed to an inch high and the greens mowed smooth to a half an inch high. Water rumbled through the centre creek and verged with another creek on the west side. A white majestic club house sat low near the west creek. Foot bridges lead from the club house across the foaming waters to the quiet of the manicured golf course.

Lush flowers bloomed along the club house walls. Fresh young bushes and trees grew in sections around the odd shaped sand traps and rolling landscape. Idle talk from men without life's burdens chasing a little ball from hole to hole.

Memories of a time before. These same happy men, ventured to a foreign country to fight for freedom. Freedom was gained at a price of lost lives. Freedom was lost for some. On their return to home and country they noticed the spoils of war. Not the devastation they inflicted on foreign people and lands but the spoils of what enjoyment they once had before the conflicts of the second world war.

Thus, the grandeur of the golf course, between rushing waters of freedom, was now in disarray in overgrown bushes surrounded by brown fields. Sand traps became hollowed holes, greens fought and lost the war to encroaching hay fields.

Water in torrents ate at the creek banks and washed away the earth that supported the foot bridges. Flowers died beneath wandering vines.

The golf course was all but forgotten to golfers of a past generation. Now it was a field of exploration for the kids from Roosevelt Street.

□ □ □ □

C.J. Redfern, the name alone inspired his future way of life. The first-time Richard had heard the name of C.J., visions of a man in a sailor suit popped into his mind. A sailor tall and skinny wearing baggy pants and a round hat cocked over a stern brow.

In later years C.J. joined the American navy. It was about the time of the Vietnam conflict. C.J. served on a battle ship in the south Pacific wearing those navel pants and a round hat cocked over a stern brow. After serving for the Americans and standing proud as a Canadian C.J. returned to Sault Ste. Marie to live and raise a family.

It is funny that back in nineteen-sixty-three Richard had viewed C.J. as a sailor. Maybe C.J. fit the part or resembled an actor that once played a sailor. In nineteen-sixty-three Richard and friends were about ten years of age. C.J. and his friends were much older at a ripe old age of seventeen.

Hanging around older kids was not a big deal. If it needed to be said, everyone needed everyone to make up teams for baseball or hockey pickup games. It was after a pickup game of twenty-one. A game of baseball where one batter hits the softball out into a field of ten or more kids. Up front were the younger kids, to the back were the older boys waiting for fly-balls worth five points. Grabbing the odd grounder for one point or a bouncer for three points a kid could earn enough points in a round to take his place as a batter.

More often the older boys made it to bat rather than the younger kids. On occasion boys C.J.'s age like Francis Hebert, David and Ralf Yanni, Tom or Jerry would hit grounders and bouncers to the younger boys.

This one day after a pickup game, when everyone became pooped out from running under the summer sun, the boys gathered in small groups to cool off on the grass. St. Francis School sat silent during the summer vacation. Most of the boys attended the school or had attended. Only a game of twenty-one would bring kids willingly back to school property.

One group of boys gathered to talk about nothing of importance. C.J., Tom, Jerry, Pat, Mark and Richard lounged on the grass each chewing coolly on a blade of green grass. C.J. carried on with most of the conversation. As usual, for a seventeen-year-old, talk revolved around girls. For Pat, Mark and Richard being the younger boys of the group they listened without comprehension.

"I tell you I saw it with my own eyes." bragged C.J. "I was right there for the whole show."

"What show?" asked an inquisitive Pat."

"And when was this?" Tom now pressured C.J. for an exact time of occurrence.

"Where was this?" pressured Jerry, he commenced to chew on a twig. "Where is this location? You are keeping this a secret just for yourself?"

Again, Pat interrupted. "What show?"

"And it happens just about this time every day." C.J. said with confidence as he stretched out onto his back. With his hands behind his neck a smile of satisfaction came to his lips."

Tom squatted between Richard and Mark edging in to make room. "I take it that you are not divulging the location?"

"I found the place. If I tell you and you then you and you will tell someone else, then they will tell someone." a pointed finger was directed towards Jerry and Tom as C.J. spoke. His finger moved towards the younger boys. "Besides, these three are too young."

"Too young for what?" questioned Mark, his eyes bright. He was asking for Pat, Richard and himself.

Richard sat there mostly listening. Like an independent observer, he observed the twig in Jerry's mouth flopping around. Pat tapped the baseball bat between his legs. Mark blew his nose into a white hanky that was no longer white. Tom with a wide wholesome grin egged an answer from C.J., who smirked with satisfaction. C.J. had something over the other boys.

"For the show." Pat quickly answered Mark's question. "I do not know what show he is talking about." Pat turned to C.J. who was beginning to smile pleasantly. "What show C.J.?"

C.J. propped himself up onto his elbows, a sunburnt line showed below his tee-shirt sleeve. "Do you guys promise not to tell anyone?"

Each guy in turn looked at the other as each head began to bob with agreement. After each one made eye contact they turned and sat crossed legged facing towards C.J. as he leaned in closer to the boys. C.J. had the cool look, Elvis hair, white socks, running shoes and wrangler jeans with a double turned cuff.

"Do you know where the old barn is across the creek?"

Jerry and Tom nodded, the other three agreed without actually knowing.

"Well, you know where the other creek is with the long bridge leading to the old golf club house."

Mark's eye balls peered out from the corner of his eye sockets. He looked at Pat who gave an I-do-not-know face and the shrugging shoulders from Richard.

"And it is about that time now that I usually take in the show."

"What show?" Pats exasperated voice asked.

C.J. gave Pat a cocked eye. "I will show you what show." he answered before Pat again asked the same repetitive question.

Up and walking away before anyone knew what was happening C.J. was heading towards a gully behind the school. Grabbing bats, balls and gloves, the boys made haste to follow.

Summer's mid day heat took a notch down as the boy's stomach's internal three o'clock warning-bell began to sound. This trip would have to be a quick one before supper time came around. If the boys were not home their would-be mothers leaned out of back boors hollering for their kids.

St. Francis School is a flat roof building with rooms on both sides of a long hallway. Behind the school was a twenty-foot gully that separated the school from the old part of the golf course. Patches of short growing green grass floated like scum in a field of brown hay. Shrub bush grew tangled intertwined to become a barrier to prevent access to the secrets that only C.J. knew about.

In single-file the boys followed C.J. through the tangled barriers, over fallen fence wire, through and around bush sitting like islands in the field. Surely C.J. was double tracking, going so far then doubling back then forward again. By all means, the younger guys were lost. It would take several outings by the three junior followers to explore this area before becoming familiar with the land's layout.

Suddenly C.J. stopped. Each guy in turn stopped. At the end of the line Richard brought up the rear bumping into Mark. Peeking around he questioned the hold up. Mark leaned to the side, Pat poked a head around Jerry.

"Okay boys we are getting close." C.J. crouched to one knee. "See that old barn over there."

All looked in the direction of C.J.'s pointed finger. Behind bush a tilted barn's front corner could be seen. Weathered grey brown dry boards seemed to creak with old age.

"That barn all locked up."

"Yeah." all acknowledged.

"There is all kinds of army stuff inside." C.J.'s voice became low. "I once made it all the way to the barn before some old guy saw me." his voice dragged slowly as the story unfolded then it quickened with excitement. "That old guy had a double barrel shotgun filled with rock salt."

Jerry interrogated C.J., a hint of doubt was in his voice. "Did he shoot you with the rock salt?"

"Missed."

Tom began to explain the purpose of rock salt. "It will not kill you but when the salt hits it stings. It will burn for days and days."

"If he hits you in the butt." announced C.J.. "you will not be able to sit down for a week."

Mark's freckled face puckered from behind the alders. "What kind of army stuff is in there?"

"Old grenades, boots, army coats and plenty of gas masks." C.J. held the attention of the boys building suspense with his words. "Would you like to see one. I bet I can sneak over there, squeeze through the door, grab a gas mask and be back here before the old man see's me."

All nodded with mischievous wonderment. Gathering closer together to hear any final details from C.J. they quoted the odds of him making it.

Crouching down on all four's C.J. began to crawl out into the opening of the field. Wild grass of the old golf course was about knee-high. Hesitating for a moment, then C.J. turned to the boys. "If the old man comes out with a loaded shotgun . . . just run as fast as you can. I will be right behind you."

On hands and knees, he crawled through the tall grass with only his head bobbing above the tops of the grass. Seeing this manner of height between the grass and C.J., Richard recalled a similar occurrence a year or two earlier. Richard's thoughts flowed in his memory back to that time.

FIELDS TO EXPLORE
CHAPTER 8
TALL GRASS

Cool nights welcomed warm hot days. The rain fell just enough to give nourishment to the earth. In Korah Township the farmers were happy when their crops were abundant. On Second Line, the main artery running east to west, the fields of hay, buck wheat and oats were tall with their grain stocks reaching for the sky.

Laura and Richard were about seven years old when they found themselves together wandering the neighborhood. Not the best of friends, just next door neighbors, kids that got along together. When there were no other kids of their gender to play with, then the two found a need to hang around together.

"I am older than you." Laura boasted. "When you get older you can be the leader."

Richard had no objection. Today he had no intention of leading anyone anywhere of importance. "Okay." his voice was too enthusiastic and compliant. Richard was just open to any interest and activity of the day.

On the other hand, Laura wearing black strapped shoes, knee-high socks and a one-piece dress, was looking for something exciting and different to do. Not mischievous or a bad kid, but Laura sure could get into life's adventures like any boy.

"Where are we going?" asked Richard as he followed Laura through McAuley's back yard then Smyth's and Sullivan's yards.

"I have to pee."

Richard stopped and looked back in the direction of Laura's house. He stood confused thinking for a moment. Only boys, as far as he knew, did not have to go home to pee. "Your house is over there."

Laura looked back in the direction of Richard's pointed finger. Her face was scrunched up. She knew where her house was. "It is too far. I have to go now."

Richard squinted up one eye and sucked in part of his lower lip. "Too, Far." he mumbled while standing watching Laura find an evergreen shrub to hide under. While waiting

Richard shoved his hands into the pockets of his jean pants. In his thoughts, he deducted that Laura could have run home to pee and run back in the amount of time it took her to find a shrub to pee under.

Sounds of water hitting the hard-dry ground caught Richard's ears. Inquisitiveness made him turn to face the shrub of cedar evergreens. That cedar smell of pungent and sweet aroma is the kind of smell that forever lingers in one's mind. Life's experiences in memory can be recalled with the occurrence of cedar smells in the air. To this day, Richard is reminded of Laura's need to pee every time he smells the aromatic cedar.

"What are you waiting for?" Laura tuned as she began heading away from the shrub. "Are you in dream land?"

He was in dream land but Richard shook his head no then began to follow with hands still deep in the pockets of his faded blue jeans.

"Do you want to go to the school?"

"No." confirmed Richard with a sound of authority. "It is summer, school is finished, I do not want to go back there."

Laura began skipping through the ragged grass that came to her waist. The Sullivan house was empty this summer. They had gone away on vacation. No one had cut the grass in the back yard for a while.

"Not to go to school. To go play at the school. The field is full of grass as tall as this." Laura pulled a stock of grass and pulled it to the middle of her chest.

"Sure." Richard's voice did not have that excitement Laura was expecting.

"It is true. I will show you."

Laura began to run through Sullivan's back yard with Richard reluctantly following. St. Francis school stood cold and quiet as if asleep or hibernating. Maybe it was resting from a year of noisy hyperactive children. Black curtains were drawn across the tall glass windows as if its eye lids were closed. North away from the school the field began. Three quarters of the way down the field tall elm trees stood in a straight line twenty feet apart. Another line of elms stood identical at the very end where second line ran east to west.

Green lush buckwheat of spring had now turned to a golden brown. Seed shells began to open on the stock stem heads. There was no wind to speak of though gently the field swayed in smooth random movements. Patterns and shapes came and vanished across the top of the field.

Laura and Richard stood on the pavement at the edge of the school yard where the cut grass tapered up to meet the buckwheat. In the distance the elm trees seemed to be sinking into a lake of wheat.

"It does not look tall at all. Not as tall as I am." said Richard feeling that his height was the greater.

"Let's see." Laura bent into a racer's stance ready to burst at the firing of a starter's pistol. "I will race you."

"Okay."

Before Richard even made ready his stance Laura burst into a run towards the tall wheat. After a hesitant step, Richard let his black canvas running shoes carry lanky legs into a full run.

Directly overhead cloudless skies let the noonday sun heat the earth. Dew from the cool night began to vaporize. A wet heat slowly rose from the field of wheat. Two kids could feel their clothes sticking to their bodies as they ran and ran. Voices called out laughing and enjoying the splendor of swimming in a field of grass.

Suddenly their energy waned and silence befell while the two kids stood still somewhere in the sea of grass. Long stems of grass rubbed against the children. Only the odd sound of a grasshopper could be heard. A low thump, thumping was the beating of their own happy hearts.

Laura was right, the grass was taller than they were. Where they were, where each other was, was unknown. They could hear but could not see each other. They knew that the school was south and Brookfield Street was east and the creek was west because the tops of the giant elms could be seen at the north end of the field.

Richard wiped a bead of sweat from his forehead. As he talked, he inspected the tall strands of grass. The many leaves, the head of the wheat and the many clusters of seeds. "Laura." he called out with the curiosity of needing to know where she was. "Laura! Where are you?"

"Over here!" Laura looked about. Here could be there, she knew she was standing on a spot but where was the spot in relationship to Richard. "Over here somewhere." She tugged at her dress that clung to her legs.

"I can hear you but I cannot see you." Bending to his knees, Richard rolled onto his back. Above the ends of the wheat seemed to tickle the light blue sky. Lifting his arms, as if he were able to touch the sky, but they were too short. Only the wheat caressed the heavens. "What are you doing Laura?"

"Taking my clothes off." she replied in a matter of fact way. With the sun's heat and the dew's moisture mixing together Laura decided the combination was too much. She pulled the flower print dress off over her head. The simple cotton underwear were next. Only the shoes and socks were left on so she would be able to run through the field.

"Taking off all of your clothes?" Then again Richard thought. 'She had done it before when she was younger.'

Through the grass, Laura ran as the blades of grass brushed against her body wiping and cooling the heated dew on her skin. Laura's laughs and giggles filled the air. Richard heard her voice coming from different places all around him. Sure, he was curious but Laura was illusive in the tall grass.

After what seemed like hours, the two voices in the field emerged onto Brookfield Road. To Richard's dismay Laura had her clothes back on.

"That was fun." exclaimed Laura. "Did you take your clothes off?"

An embarrassed Richard shook his head no.

"We should come here tomorrow and do it again. This time you can take your clothes off too." Laura skipped down the road excited about tomorrow's plan.

Richard followed, not skipping but walking confused, as he tucked his shirt tail into his pants. For several days, he waited for Laura to suggest going to the field. Days passed into a week. One day while wandering Richard stopped by the school and stood on the edge of the asphalt and stared at the far away elm trees. There they stood even taller than he remembered. Could it have been due to the lack of grass? Gone from the field was the tall buckwheat. Gone was the chance for Laura and himself to run naked through the tickling blades of summer's grass.

FIELDS TO EXPLORE
CHAPTER 9
GAS MASK

All eyes were keeping a lookout for anything of surprise especially the old man with the shotgun loaded with rock salt. C.J. had made it, he stood leaning against the corner of the weathered barn. There was an extra silence surrounding the area. The boy's hearts seemed to beat louder. Birds in the trees chirped softer as if they too anticipated the blast from the old man's shotgun.

C.J. gave an okay sign with his hand. He leaned back against the barn as he peeked his head around the corner. The coast seemed safe, all was clear.

"He is almost there." Tom informed everyone.

The boys could see that C.J. was almost there but Tom needed to confirm the situation just to calm his own anxiety. Even the wind ceased to blow. Leaves on the trees stopped fluttering. Everyone and everything held their breath as C.J. made his move. Edging against the dry barn board he moved from the side to the front then to the barn doors. They stood slightly ajar at the bottom. An old lock on a rusty hasp held the plank doors latched. Being old and flimsy gave play to the aged wood. A gap at the bottom allowed C.J. to crawl into the darkness of the barn.

"If the old man shows up how do we warn C.J.?" asked Pat of his older brother Tom. Brothers of slim features and blonde hair looked more like twins. Tom was the older of the two but Pat seemed inching to be taller.

"We just...." Tom paused to think. ". . . holler then run. The old man will hear us and come after us. C.J. can then sneak out and get away."

"Run like hell." added Jerry.

Everyone changed position into a semi crouch with feet ready to speed away. Mark and Richard who were beginning to crouch stepped slightly to the side. If there was a sudden need to run, both did not want to be trampled by the others.

All eyes were glued on the barn. C.J. was sure taking his sweet time inside of the barn, so it seemed to the boys. Minute after minute passed with agitation, tension was building in the muscles of legs and feet.

"Do you think C.J. is okay?" questioned a concerned Mark.

"Maybe the old man is inside."

"The old man captured C.J."

"No, C.J. would have made a run for it." Tom answered back to Pat and Jerry. "C.J. is not afraid of a little rock salt. It just stings for a while."

First came C.J.'s head as if he was first being born then his hips and legs. Quickly he made a zig-zag sprint towards the waiting guys. In one unplanned motion the boys turned and high-tailed it along the path with C.J. hot behind their retreat.

Back through the bush, across the short grass, through the tangled alders to another section of depressions in the field lacking sand. With panting breaths, the boys flopped onto the ground around the depression. They were joyful that they had made it safe and without rock salt being shot at them.

C.J. held out the object of their quest. One after another each inspected the world war two gas mask. From the greenish grey rubber, to the droopy large eye lenses, to the air filters that resembled large nostrils from an extinct sea creature, each boy inspected the gas mask.

All had touched and put the gas mask on. Each boy created a character to display. Mark bobbed up and down, Pat swam like a fish in the sand depression, Richard staggered struggling to breath in fresh air before falling to the ground. Each boy breathed in through the mask then passed out.

"Bad air." gasped Jerry.

Innocent of the real tragedies of the war the boys made light of what their fathers might have gone through during the dark years of battle. Years later only C.J. would get a taste of what war was like. Here and now life and the games they played was just play.

"I have to take a wicked pee." Jerry informed the others.

"Me too." seconded Pat.

With all of the excitement it was bound to increase the need to pee. Luck had it that no one pee'ed them-selves before or during the retreat. Now after the adventure all needed to relieve them-selves in a big way.

"Who has to go real-bad?" Tom was looking for conformation.

Just the suggestion, of needing to go, made those that did not have to pee, think of needing to pee. Everyone raised their hands. Pat squeezed his knees together and stepped from foot to foot.

□□□□□

"I think Pat really has to go." teased C.J.. "I think he is going to pee his pants."

"No, I'm not. I do not pee my pants."

"Yes, you will if I tickle you." C.J. lunged towards Pat who in turn scrambled behind his brother. "I bet I can make you pee your pants."

Mark and Richard stood tall and stiff without fidgeting. Both boys had to pee and pee bad. It was their best defense to not show signs of needing to pee. They would not be able to withstand the torturing of being tickled.

Jerry joined in on the chase with C.J. after an evasive Pat. On the escape, Pat ran, jumped, rolled and leaped like a slippery frog. Almost to the point of capture Tom came to brother Pat's rescue.

"Let's start a grass fire in this sand pit and see if we are able to put it out without fire hoses."

C.J. and Jerry looked towards each other then at Pat, who they now had pinned to the ground. In panic Pat nodded his head frantically for leniency.

"Okay." announced Jerry and C.J. as they left Pat squirming on the ground.

Tom gathered loose dry grass into a pile in the sand depression that was once the golf course sand-trap. When the pile was large-enough Tom pulled penny matches from his pocket. After the second match stick sparked into a flame of yellow and blue burning sulfur, Tom set the grass aflame.

"Wait until I say now." Tom insisted. "Wait until the fire is really going.

Standing around the edge of the pit, the boys leaned forward with their fire hoses pointing towards the building flame. Bladders were filled to the brim, muscles tensed trying to refrain from peeing too soon. If one pee`ed before the order to 'go' they would be labeled a wimp, a sissy. Leg muscles began to quiver, minds tried to think of something different, eyes began to water. Fingers squeezed their fire hoses to hold back the built-up water pressure.

"Now!" yelled Tom as he no longer could restrain the pressure.

The fire had no chance to survive. From all sides the flames were attacked by miniature fire hoses with an over abundance of water. Within seconds the fire smoldered out with the odd fellow shaking the last drop from a relieved bladder.

"Not bad." praised Tom. With relief, he stretched out on the ground and stared skyward. "We could have put out an even bigger fire."

All agreed as they in turn zipped up and stored their hoses. Relaxing they soaked up the summer sun's warmth.

"What about the show?" asked Pat just when the silent group was relaxed.

FIELDS TO EXPLORE
CHAPTER 10
THE SHOW

C.J. had almost forgotten about the show. Maybe he wanted to forget. If everyone knew about the show, then the hidden viewing site would be crowded. If that happened, then C.J. would be crowed out. Laying on his back watching wispy clouds float by C.J. hesitated a moment longer.

Following the leader everyone stood after Tom got up. C.J. felt the eyes of everyone staring down upon him. He tried not to notice but reluctantly looked them all in the eyes.

"All right I will show you the spot." C.J. stood pointing a finger directly at each boy. "No on tells. This secret does not go beyond us."

Quickly everyone's head bobbed up and down. Pat continued bobbing his head after the others had stopped. Tom placed his hand under Pat's chin to halt the motion. Pat rolled his eyes smiling with a teasing grin.

"This way then." C.J. turned back towards the barn but took a different path that circled the area to take them towards the creek.

Through alders, across the field of short green grass and vacant sand traps, the boys followed single-file behind their leader. Increasing thunder began to build just beyond the hardwood trees of maple and birch growing on a slow slope that reached for the sky. Evergreen trees formed a buffer between the creek and the hardwood trees. At each closer step the roar of rushing water over a rock wall increased in volume. C.J.'s words of information was lost to the boys at the back of the line.

"What?"

"What?"

"What?" asked Richard after Mark and Pat had asked the same question.

At the ridge of the hill overlooking the creek C.J. lowered himself onto his belly. "It is just over this small hill. We have to crawl so no one will see us."

Like a secret combat mission each would-be soldier dropped to their bellies to begin the crawl through the woods. Each hand placed in front of the other followed by a slither of the body was carefully made. Silence was a must, according to C.J.'s hand gestures. No more than twenty feet of hill remained until the boys would be able to peer over the crest of the mound.

What a sight waited for those that had not seen the once glamourous grounds of the golf clubhouse area. Even now after years of neglect the place held an awesome beauty. Once manicured shrubs, plants and grass now were growing wild and spreading gaining their freedom.

All eyes scanned the grounds laying across the creek and sitting low on a delta between the two meeting creeks. Heads rested on their intertwined hands. Time lingered while eyes brought the scene to memory. C.J. pointed in different directions. All looked without understanding what they were to view.

But what a sight. A two-story white building with vines clinging to it's walls and roof sat silent between the creeks. Plants flowered at the foot of walls interrupted by bushy evergreen shrubs. Around the building leading across dark green grass, a foot path leads to a suspension bridge crossing the creek below in front of the boys. Steel grey cables stretched from side to side and sagged in the middle from the bridge's own weight.

Once white painted boards planked the walkway of the bridge. Handrails of faded white weaved between cables on both sides of the bridge. Below the slightly swaying bridge the rushing clean water gave an inclination of an optical illusion. The bridge seemed to be floating sideways along with the creek's flow yet never moving from its anchored position.

C.J.'s whispered voice was lost under the echoing sounds of rushing water. As he talked C.J. continued to point towards a green box at the back of the building. Near a door an open box was supported by four posts. The height of the box was approximately three feet high and about a foot and a half up from the ground.

"She comes out every day about this time to take a shower." C.J. lifted his head as if to peek over the top of the box. "From this height, I can see almost everything over the top of the shower box."

All lifted their heads to look into the empty box.

Tom strained his voice as he stretched his neck. "Where does she change?"

"She comes out wrapped in a towel and takes it off before she gets into the shower."

Tom and Jerry looked at C.J. with excited eyes and adolescent hormonal thoughts roving in their minds. Pat, Mark and Richard being younger continued to stare at the shower waiting to see what the big deal was all about. Adolescent hormones had not quite reached the boy's activation switch.

"Where is she today?" Jerry asked impatiently. The twig he chewed on moved faster from side to side. "I do not think she is home. Does anyone actually live there?"

"She lives there. I have seen her . . . plenty of times." C.J. tied to back up his words with facts. "The lawn is cut. Look, the garden on the side of the house is growing."

Jerry and Tom gave a half-attempted nod. Tom continued to stretch his neck for a better view. With the twig moving faster from side to side Jerry stood up.

"Maybe she has already took a shower, or she is working late." C.J. had lost his edge, his evidence had not made an appearance. "I tell you she is stacked. Too bad we missed her."

Reluctantly one by one each boy stood, stretched, put their hands in pants' pockets, kicked at the ground and wandered off to explore the surrounding area. Soon their internal clocks reminded them that supper was waiting and it was time to go home.

Each evening between five and six o'clock a country and western show would play on the radio. A theme song would play at the start and end of the show. A song that sticks in one's mind over the years when one thinks of the suppertime meal.

"Come Home, Come Home it's suppertime."

Between chatter the boys headed down the hill leaving the valley scene to be swallowed by the roar of water. Home and supper was calling them.

"Maybe next time." assured C.J.

Over the years, the banks were washed away by the creeks. One year the club house just vanished, it was there then gone. Jerry and Richard explored the area sometimes playing and fishing from the swaying bridge. Then one spring it too had disappeared with the rushing high water and into one's memory.

No one had ever mentioned if they had revisited the house when it was still there, or claimed that they had seen a free show.

SPORTS
CHAPTER 11
MUD BOMBS

It was about the time that Richard and his family moved. They were moving but not all that far away. Richard was just turning ten years of age at the time and as they say 'sprouting like a bad weed'. The expression was about a bad weed not directed to Richard as a person.

Mr. And Mrs. Dewer were moving back to Korah Township and to their home. Mrs. Irene Dewer was an aunt of Mrs. Georgette Mousseau. The Dewer's had rented the house to Fern and Georgette Mousseau. After working up along the A.C.R. rail line the Dewer's decided to move back home.

Well the Mousseau's now needed to move. Fern looked around house hunting and searching for a new home for his family. A house came up for sale just down the street near the middle at the intersection of Balfour and Roosevelt Streets. Mr. and Mrs. Hall were moving to a newer and larger house. Within a month of knowing they were moving Richard found himself in a new house, a new bedroom and new adventures.

Nineteen-sixty-one was a year of change. Mark and Richard were still best friends. As friends go, when growing up, one hangs around with new friends for a while. This beginning of summer Jerry and Richard began to hang around together. Mark and his family had gone on a traveling vacation. It would be a bit of a change as far as playing experiences go. Though all kids played games together, old and young, boys and girls it would be a little different when only two are seeking adventure. Jerry was a couple of years older than Richard but in height and size Richard was his equal. This summer's adventures would be a little different in scope.

Leaving the house once lived in for almost ten years felt strange for Richard. After the first night in the new house the past was forgotten. That white two-story house, with a staircase leading upstairs to the bedrooms and bath, the basement where the puffing furnace ate coal and wood, was almost forgotten at the upper end of Roosevelt Street. It was as if it was no longer his and not being able to visit an old friend. Somehow friends at the upper end were almost as forgotten as the house.

In the new one story house with blue slate siding Richard's bedroom was now in the basement. Things were sure different and it took awhile to feel at home. For sometime Richard did not seem to wander as much, rather preferring to stick around his new home. There were his brothers' Donald and Marc to play within the sand pit located in the back yard. There was a new little sister they were told would be arriving soon. When sister Terri-Lynn did arrive in person, it was no big deal for the boys. After all she was too small to play in the sand pit.

Jerry was the first to venture down the street to see how things were going. Chumming around began as they hung around the sand pit. Jerry knew young Walter next door to Richard's house. Walter was between the ages of Jerry and Richard.

Unlike the kids of today, board with life because of lack of imagination, the boys did know how to play. Everyone on the street regardless of age knew how to play and have fun.

Walter was of heavy set, not fat, thick muscles on a stocky frame. Wisps of light brown hair floated on the top of his head combed from left to right. This was the style of the generation until the Beatles arrived with their influences. It would take awhile for the styles to reach Roosevelt Street but it eventually did.

Jerry and Richard stayed on the skinny side of body weight. Hair wise, well Jerry's was light and thin. Later in life to be thinned right out when he was older. Richard was one of the lucky ones to retain a full head of hair. Jerry liked to chew on a twig even when there was no twig in his mouth.

I guess Richard needed friends like Jerry and Walter at the time. Richard was always quiet, more of a follower and an observer. He was not one to be lead astray or into doing wrong. Being shy and not saying much Richard would leave that to others. He held his own at times when confronted or challenged. Challenging the need to get a haircut was never successful. Dad took the three boys for a well-needed brush-cut for the coming hot days of summer.

□□□□

Spring had brought enough rain to soak and saturate the ground for weeks. All of the creeks were swollen to the brim. Around Roosevelt Street and the surrounding area, the base of earth was clay with a thin layer of loam about two feet thick. At the time during the ice age when the great lakes were being formed the St. Mary's river was carved out to drain Lake Superior's water into Lake Huron. Over centuries the river valley narrowed and narrowed leaving a sliver of water between silted flat land bounded by ridges of Canadian shield rock.

Above the deep bed rock of the valley was left the hard clay. Hard clay until it was exposed to water. Semi-solid goo flowed, stuck to things then swallowed them never to be seen again. All the creeks around the neighborhood flooded with rushing water from heavy rains. So strong and willful were the depths of water that creeks changed paths, ate away banks swallowing whole tree roots and branches.

That year most of the land around the old golf course clubhouse was swallowed up. Contractors took the rest away in pieces shoveled into dump trucks. On several occasions the boys visited the area and the old barn. With the clubhouse gone the boys figured the old man with the shotgun loaded with rock salt would also be gone.

A rusted pad lock occupied the frame of the weathered and rotting doors. Along the ground around the barn's walls there were boards missing. Most were rotten away. Each boy in turn made his way to the barn peeking in or wiggling between the loose openings of the doors. Gone were the army surpluses from the war years. Only bits and pieces of rubber gas masks lay on the ground. A planed fire by the owners or people in charge reduced memories into grey ashes. Green grass outlined the barn's area that summer. New grass the following year erased its existence for future explorers.

Jerry, Walter and Richard sat on the swaying bridge for the last time that summer. The following year it too disappeared. All of the land around the old golf course had changed. All things in life continue to change whether we want time to stand still or always be the way we remember.

□□□□

"Where to now?" Walter asked. He and the boys stood on the bank of the creek. "There is nothing here."

Jerry and Richard nodded with disappointed agreement. The golf course clubhouse was gone, the barn was gone. Turning around they crossed the swing bridge for the last time.

"Where to now?"

"We can follow the creek and see where it goes."

suggested Jerry, he picked up a twig to chew on.

The statement was not up for debate. Why would there be a need to discuss where and why they needed to follow the creek?

Away they went along the bank of the creek. Shear cliffs had funneled the creek along its path. Earth, roots and shrubs hung over the edge as if ripped away. Clay beneath glistened with a wet glaze. Fifteen feet was cut from the banks leaving clay walls and a creek trickling below.

Richard leaned over the bank testing his bravery. Below the water did not seem all that deep or fast. He stepped a foot back from the edge dropping a ball sized rock. A hollow thud sounded as the rock plunged into two feet of deep water. This assured Richard and most likely the others that the water was still dangerous. Continuing along the creek the boys wandered aimlessly tossing rocks and stones into the water. Play was just whiling away the hours with nothing of importance to accomplish.

Spring rains combined with heavy run-off of winter snows had cut a wide and deep path through the creek bed. Near the end of the school yard where the creek made a bend at Mr. Allen's farm, the creek bank made a wide curve doubling back on its self. A clay hill jutted out with the creek circling three quarters of the way around.

"I hear something." Walter froze in mid steps. "I think I hear some voices."

Jerry strained to hear over the echoing water flow. "I do not hear anything."

"I think it is coming from that side of the creek." Pointing in a curve Walter covered a section of area across the creek.

"Let's sneak up on them and see what they are doing." Richard crouched as he lowered his voice. "We have to get across the creek."

Sneaking their way through the bush, they made their way to the water and crossed on fallen trees that had bunched up on a low spot in the creek. Voices became louder the closer they came to the crest of the opposite creek bank. Three heads popped over the top layer of the sod to see four boys sliding down the wet clay of the hill.

"I only know one of those guys." said Walter.

Richard answered with pride. "That is Alfred, a friend of mine. He is in my class."

"Who are those guys he is with? They do not come from around our streets." Jerry made note. "Alfred lives two streets over from us near the public school."

Walter leaned up to get a better look. "Yeah, maybe they go to the public school and just hang around that area."

"Maybe Alfred is showing them around our neck of the woods." Richard tried to grab a better foot hold in the slippery clay. "We know Alfred, so lets go join them."

It is funny how streets can separate people. Public and separate school kids did not hang around together. Kids are kids and there are no political or religious reasons why kids should not play together. Canada is not Ireland where children are imprinted to dislike each other by parents of parents of parents that created a religious disagreement of no importance.

Here in Canada, in Sault Ste. Marie on Roosevelt Street in Korah Township, just streets kept kids from playing with kids from several streets over. Not religion, schools, ancestors, nationality or political reasons that prevented kids from associating. Just distance from one street to another kept kids apart.

Feet pushed and kicked their way over the bank of slippery clay. Hands grabbed at the roots to haul bodies up. Jerry, Walter and Richard made their way down the bank and over towards the new boys sliding down the slick clay. Alfred called out hi as he slid by on the seat of his pants. Without need for introductions the three joined in on the fun.

Hands, feet, and knees grabbed and kicked their way to the top of the twenty-foot bank. Puffing from exertion down they slid with laughter that drained their strength.

"Splat!"

"Which one of you guys did that?" Walter turned to look down to the bottom of the hill. "Who threw the mud pie?" Turning his head to try and see the back of his shirt Walter spun around like a dog chasing its tail.

Everyone stood there, shrugging shoulders and keeping an eye on Jerry, the true culprit. When Walter turned to look over his shoulder Jerry, the true culprit, nodded. Quickly the boys grabbed a handful of yellow wet clay and heaved with all their might towards Walter at the top of the hill.

"Splat, a thud, splat!"

There was no mistaking who was tossing the mud pies. Walter tried to duck and dodge but failed as several mud pies forced him over the opposite edge. Down to the bottom slipping and sliding Walter clamber back to the top of the hill.

"So, that is it eh." yelled Walter as he stood to face his attackers below. "You are all going to gang up on me?"

"Heck no." Jerry yelled back with forced honesty. "You are our friend, come on down."

Walter hesitated then sat on the edge and pushed off on a slide to the bottom bombarded by a hail of new mud pies. "Splat, splat!"

Jerry looked at the others then at Walter and said with a playfulness in his voice. "Just because you were there."

"Thanks."

"Care for a mud fight?" a dark-haired boy asked.

A mud fight, sure a mud fight would be okay. Snowball fights in the winter were okay. Boys and girls from one yard to another, from one side of the street to the other, snowballs exploded when they landed. Sometimes snow-forts, castle walls were built ten feet apart for a friendly game of war. Serious snowball fighters would stockpile their ammo and work all day and evening to be ready for the next day's encounter. No one ever really won.

A mud fight would not be any different. Two sides tossing soupy clumps of clay that would then splat and explode. It was just wet clay that would dry under the afternoon sun. So, the boys would have to take an extra bath this week. A bath would not tarnish their image.

"You guys against us." stated the other boy from Alfred's street. "The visitors against the home team."

Richard nodded. "What about Alfred, he is a home team player but lives near you guys?"

"I will be on the visitor's team." Alfred stepped next to the other boys. "It will be more fair if I help the three visitors."

"Sounds good."

"Okay by me."

"Settled."

All nodded and verbally made a gentleman's agreement. After all it was just a friendly snowball game of war, in the summer time, with mud pie bombs.

Rules of war, according to the Roosevelt Street Convention had been made. Jerry already had bent down to grab a handful of the earth's wet clay. All three boys on the visiting team hesitated as if waiting for a run for it command. Something registered in their minds when Jerry's actions convinced them to run for cover. Rubber soles on canvas running shoes slipped and inched the boy's ascent up the clay hill. At any moment, an anticipated splat of cool clay was inevitable. Being an honest adversary Jerry waited until the last of the enemy's butt had crested the hill.

"Fire." sounded Jerry's loud voice with a hint of playful excitement.

A volley of clay globs sailed in an arc over the hill destined for enemy bodies that surely were busy forming counter attack globs of clay.

"Incoming." warned Walter, he ducked away from a soupy splat of clay. "Duck and move."

Alfred and company bombarded the home team from their high vantage point. As quick as hands were able to grab the clay, another bombardment was hailed upon the home team. Out in the open and at the bottom of the hill Richard, Walter and Jerry stood out like clay pigeons waiting to be knocked over.

"Head for cover." Jerry yelled. Time was instant as a clay splat of earth hit between his shoulders. "Ahhh . . ., head for that hill." Jerry pointed to the sod-covered hill jutting out from the creek's side.

Bodies scrambled up and over the small hill. Walter lobbed a large glob into a high arc that seemed to hang in mid air as if frozen in time. There was no time to admire one's projectile sailing through the air towards its intended destination. Hands were busy removing ammo from the earth then rapidly sending it towards a new destination.

In a time of peace when games of fun imitate real life do children think of real scenarios or consequences? Richard's dad was under age when the second world war began. Walter's dad was stationed up in the Yukon building defense buildings. Jerry's dad had seen a little action. All of the kids on Roosevelt Street had dads that came back physically okay. No one thought or asked of their emotional state.

"Incoming." Alfred's voice carried over the yells and hoots that the other boys vocalized. "Ahhh . . ., I am hit." yelled Alfred after a direct splat to the top of his forehead.

"Good shot." Walter and Richard complemented Jerry for the group's first direct hit.

Soupy clay dripped over Alfred's eyes, nose and mouth. With one hand to clear his sight Alfred's other hand was busy rapidly tossing palm sized balls towards the enemy, his friends.

By the time a truce was called, because of the time being near the supper hour, the boys wore the tell-tale signs of their embattlement. Each boy looked the other over and attempted to count the number of clay hits.

"Well . . .," pondered Walter as he began to note his findings. "your guy and Richard seem to be the cleanest so I guess it is a tie."

Both teams nodded their heads in agreement, no losers, no winners. This war game had everyone walking away happy and free of injury.

"That one hit me clean on the head."

"That is nothing Alfred." Walter pointed to the back of his neck. "Two big ones right here."

"I tasted that one you threw at me." pointed out Alfred's friend to Jerry.

Pulling his tee-shirt collar forward Jerry revealed the results of his wounds. "Look more went down my shirt." Jerry lifted the tail of the tee-shirt from his pants to let drying clay fall to the street.

Walking slightly behind the others and slightly cleaner Richard and a friendly enemy walked together without saying much. Once in awhile they looked each other over and nodded. A smile indicated that they had experienced fun. What more needs to be said.

"I think you got me in the side." A boy pointed to his left side under the arm.

Richard leaned as he walked. "You got me in the leg." He pointed with a bit of pride.

The boy from the next street over took a closer look and nodded with agreement.

At the corner of the street the teams parted with hearts happy and minds filled with innocent memories.

SPORTS
CHAPTER 12
BIRD HUNTING

Summer's heat hovered over the neighborhood unlike a cloud of condensed heat waves. Clothes stuck to the bodies like glue. Air conditioning was a fan of crimped newspaper being vibrated feverishly against stagnate airs. No one moved about in the early mornings. Sluggishly mothers, fathers and children edged into the day as the sun climbed into the sky with white-hot rays of heat. Humidity to a kid is a sprinkler in someone's yard that invites a run through, then it was onto the next yard.

Jerry and Richard were making their way down Roosevelt Street before the summer's sun's rays cleared the tree tops. Through one sprinkler at a run then through the next inching along as slow as a snail. To beat the arcing water at a slow walk before the sprinkler rotated over was a game. Even if one happed to beat the sprinkler before one left it was a must to return and run through the heaviest drops of water.

As dead calm as the humid heat the sleepy neighborhood siphoned another moment of needed shut-eye. Why? The best part of the day was the early morning. Jerry and Richard had planned to make the best of the day.

After raiding the McAuley's garden during the previous evening the two camped out in Richard's back yard planning their coming events. Shelled pea shells piled up in the centre of the tent. A sweet vegetable aroma fought the mildew of the old canvas tent. Richard held onto every word Jerry spoke. Jerry was older by a couple of years. He had lived more and had more stories. A quiet and studied person Richard drew in every word. To learn one must listen.

"This is a one-ten caliber pellet air rifle." said Jerry as he wiped the black barrel with a small piece of oiled rag. "The more you pump the cylinder the more power you can get." Jerry grunted as he repeatedly cranked the rifle in half until he could no longer bend the lever. "There, that is full power."

Under the dim light of the moon shining through the faded white canvas of the tent Richard leaned forward to observe Jerry's instructions. Another shelled pea was popped into his mouth with the casing added to the mounting pile.

"There is no pellet in the chamber. That is the part here at the start of the barrel." Jerry pointed to the place then shouldered the rifle and aimed it towards the silhouette of the moon on the canvas ceiling. A pop of air sounded, a silent pop not a loud explosion which Richard was expecting.

"Is that all the sound it makes?"

"Yeah, but the power is there. It can break a pop bottle." Jerry emphasized the point. "Break a pop bottle." Under his sleeping bag Jerry placed the rifle. "With this rifle I could get us breakfast. Tomorrow morning I will get us breakfast. We will need a fire to cook our food. You get some matches."

Richard nodded with anticipated excitement. With a thumb pressed against a huge pea shell Richard slid this thumb through the shell. A row of peas popped into his mouth with a cool fresh taste savoring between crunching teeth.

Under the cloak of heavy dew beginning to rise with the morning heat Jerry and Richard stood facing the old garage ready to release the night's held water. After retrieving the matches from the house the two were off on the morning hunt. A right of passage for all boys to become hunter gathers for their families. At fourteen, Jerry was teaching his experiences to an eleven-year-old Richard.

After several passages under and over sprinklers and a quick face wash, the boys entered lush green forest at the south end of Roosevelt Street. Above began the heat of the day. Within the bush a cool fresh smell emitted. Sounds of nature, wild creature sounds were coming from the ground, behind trees and under every leaf. Snails, worms, bugs to birds were in abundance to eyes that were willing to open and observe.

Crouching to a bended knee walk, Jerry began to lead the way with his brow in a searching frown. Every other step was hesitant. Jerry would stop, listen, look, then make another silent step. Following behind at a slow pace Richard watched every move Jerry made as he studied the art of the hunter's stalk. In silence Richard observed a ground snail motionlessly move. Small white and brown chickadees moved from branch to branch in search of their breakfast. A caw from a raven passed overhead as several blackbirds dive-bombed the raven in a playful game of tag. Early morning dew glistened on a spider's weaved webs. A night time's work paid off in the form of a small moth tangled in the web of silken strands.

Inching closer to its catch a light brown spider stalked its catch. Jerry brushed the twig that held the web. With speed the spider retreated to its hiding spot. Jerry pointed a finger skyward halting his follower then directed his finger towards an object. Richard's brown eyes widened in anticipation of seeing Jerry's intended pray.

"A rabbit's trail." whispered Jerry. "Let's follow it."

He pointed the rifle barrel in the direction intended to be taken.

A rabbit on a spit roasting over a fire just like the cowboys did in the movies. Would they be lucky enough to see a rabbit this morning? Who was going to skin and gut the furry rabbit? Richard did not know how to do it. That part they never showed in the movies. Did Jerry know?

Last night's snack of peas was beginning to ware off, it was way past breakfast time. With the sun making its way higher into the sky its heat waves were beginning to warm the forest into a humid heat. The trail lead the boys to the creek for a chance to drink and splash water onto their faces. There on the creek bank Jerry and Richard rested.

"I guess the rabbits are sleeping today." said a disappointed Jerry. "I think we will have to go after something else."

Richard sounded a sigh of relief inside knowing that he was safe from the possible embarrassment of having to skin and gut a rabbit in front of Jerry. Even though Richard was as tall and weighed as much as Jerry he looked up to the older boy as if he was a big brother. Richard was the big brother to brothers' Marc and Donald in his family. It was nice to have Jerry as a kind of an-on-loan big brother. Everyone needs someone to follow, to learn things from. Even someone older needs a younger follower to pass down knowledge to, it feels good. If asked no one would ever admit it after all men were men who did not show emotions.

"Richard, see there in the sand." pointed Jerry with a stick to the imprints in the damp sand of the creek's bank. "Look, those are rabbit prints and a raven walked here and so did a dog. The dog was probably after the rabbit."

A mental note was made in Richard's mind. He memorized the shapes and sizes of each and which belonged to which animal. The next time animal prints were found he would be able to silently gloat about impressing Jerry with his new found knowledge.

"What are we going after now Jerry?" Richard hoped it was not an animal he knew nothing about.

"Well, there are plenty of birds around." replied Jerry while he commenced an inspection of his pellet rifle. "I think I can hit a small bird." Braking open the rifle he removed the soft lead pellet then pumped the reserve chamber full of compressed air. "There a full charge." Placing the pellet back into the chamber Jerry closed the breach and pressed the safety button on. "Let's go."

Up and along the creek bank the two breakfast-hungry boys headed into the wilds of the bush. Silently along they proceeded as the minutes passed into hours. As the heat progressed, the abundance of game lessened. Richard pointed out several nice looking birds but Jerry declined with a shake of his head. There must have been a specific type and size of a bird that Jerry sought.

While Richard was beginning to loose interest and started to think of a bowl of porridge with brown sugar and cream Jerry suddenly stopped to shoulder his rifle. With the rifle butt pressed tight under his chin a pop of air, no louder than a bottle cap being removed from a twelve-cent bottle of cream soda, sounded ever so briefly. As silently a pale coloured robin fell from its perch to the cool ground below.

Richard had missed everything within a blink of an eye. It happened so quickly and finite. Hovering over their kill Jerry and Richard crouched closer to the limp body. The bird was small with no sign of the exuberant life that it once had. Did every hunter from the cave man to modern man show dismay over their actions? Surely their bounty was held in reverence, after all man survives on the nourishment that nature supplies.

For several moments eyes of the two boys watched the lifeless body of the tiny robin. All around in the surrounding forest there was a silence as if the wild creatures knew of the death of one of their own.

"There is our breakfast." stated Jerry through words that seemed apologetic. "My dad said, ' if you shoot something you have to eat it'."

Richard nodded his head while he glanced from the small bird to Jerry. A bead of sweat beneath Richard's hairline suddenly felt cold.

68

"My dad said it is against the law to waste food." Jerry picked the robin up by its legs and placed it closer to Richard. "You pluck the bird and I will get the fire going."

Hesitation prevailed as Richard stood over the bird. Jerry began to gather twigs for a fire. "Okay." answered Richard. After watching Mr. McAuley pluck chickens he felt confident that he could pluck a small chicken about the size of the robin. With fingers as nimble as a surgeon Richard began plucking the feathers until a white form lay waiting for Jerry's fire.

A small fire was coming along fine. Smoke had dissipated leaving hot coals and flames in a ten-inch pit. Taking out a small pocket knife Jerry took the bird to the creek to gut and wash in the cold water. On a sharpened stick placed through the bird it was laid to roast over the small fire.

"It smells just like chicken." noted Richard sniffing the air. "I hope that it tastes as good as chicken."

"Sure, all birds are the same. Some are big and some are small." Jerry roasted the bird slowly and talked at the same speed. "Ducks taste different than chickens and turkey taste different than a partridge."

Richard eyed the rotating bird, the skin was now a golden brown. "Is it almost ready?" It had been a long time since the snack last night of shelled peas. Hunger sounds gurgled in his belly.

Those same gurgling sounds echoed from Jerry's belly. "I am sure hungry." He brought the roasting bird closer between Richard and himself. "Here, take a piece." Jerry pulled a small piece off as did Richard. "Not bad."

The aroma tantalized their noses. To experience life is to live life and try whatever life has to offer. The bird did not taste like chicken, maybe it was not cooked enough. Neither Jerry nor Richard commented on the taste. Over the fire the bird was rotated as the flames heated the bird and the stick. With dismay or relief both boys watched the stick crack and drop the bird into the fire.

"There goes breakfast."

"And lunch." added Richard. "The sun is straight up in the sky. We missed lunch at home by now."

"I know where we can get some rhubarb to eat. It is good to eat. You dab it into brown sugar and eat it just like that."

"Okay, where do we find rhubarb Jerry?"

"By Mr. Redfern's hedge." Jerry covered the fire and bird with wet sand then stamped it down with his foot.

Just a little diversion from the planned morning breakfast. Up Roosevelt Street Jerry and Richard headed to gather breakfast and lunch from the green gardens that mother nature provided and families tended in their back yards.

SPORTS
CHAPTER 13
STREET HOCKEY

It seems that the summer months of July and August tend to last forever, only when you are a kid. Then when the first of September arrives on that first day of school summer has passed in a blink of an eye. Those warm afternoons and weekends, that sometimes linger, are used up to the fullest by eager kids full of energy.

Just when one thinks that there is yet another summer day tomorrow, wham!, Cold mornings. Heavier coats are taken out. There is less afternoon light with a hint of frost in the air. Summer is forgotten quickly when there is hockey night in Canada. Television sets are turned to the local C.B.C. station affiliate on a Saturday night.

With the best of antennas most television sets on Roosevelt Street were barely able to pick up three stations, one Canadian and two American. On Saturday night only Canadian stations carried the hockey games. A six team league, the originals. Every kid knew the teams, players and stats. Two Canadian teams battling the other American teams. Our teams ruled even with the grudge between the Toronto Maple Leafs and the Montreal Canadians. Richard and his dad were staunch Montreal fans unless they were eliminated from the playoffs. Dad then would follow the Leafs. If the leafs ended up being eliminated then the importance of the game lost it's edge. No matter who was playing hockey the game was important on a Saturday night.

It was always important to beat the Chicago Black Hawks, Boston Burins, New York Rangers and the Detroit Red Wings. Those team names conjure up history and heroes. It was a Canadian game with Canadians playing on American Teams. Oh Saturday night, the anticipation of the game. Energy flowed from every dad sitting in front of the television with sons by their sides. Sons dreamed of someday becoming the hockey stars of the future. Hockey players with mugs grinning toothless, scars majestically and somewhat proudly displayed. Every kid wished as fathers silently hoped that someday his kid would be seeking the wonder of playing professional hockey.

Saturday nights, every Saturday night in the hockey season felt the same. In every house supper ended, young children were put to bed, dads would pour a beer then wait. In anticipation of the Saturday night hockey game he would sit and wait. Why? I still wonder today why every father just sat waiting and saying. "I wonder what the score is?" For the wonderment of history let it be known that only in Canada would the powers to be waited until the finish of the first period until they would start the live broadcast.

"What is the score?" questioned Dad.

"Who is winning?" asked Richard from the comfort of the family couch.

Dad sat in the arm chair half sitting half ready to jump right into the fourteen-inch screen. Dad yelled at the players, the referee and the broad casters for every mistake that hindered his team from winning.

"What is the score?" again dad asked. "It is already past eight o'clock. What is the first period score?"

Every Saturday night was the same ritual until the broad casters quoted the score. There on the edge of his seat Dad would swear at the television in French so that the children would not understand. By some logic, it was okay to swear in French.

Across the blurred static of the black and white screen skated the heroes of hockey. In an age of reminiscence one longs to see the likes of Rocket Richard, the Pocket Richard, Beleveau or Mahovolich, Makita and Hull with Howe skating across the little static covered screen. Gump Worsley and Plante making spectacular saves, you could hear the voice of Foster Huitt's voice rising to a crescendo with colour play by play action. At home eyes that were glued to the flickering picture waged a war of conflict. Was the puck in or out of the net. A pause then Huitt's voice repeated a quote and forever lasting phrase of words. "He shots, he scores."

Heavy eye lids closed, a head rested on the couch's arm, ears working overtime filtering the volume down. Still the sounds of hockey on television entered the mind of a child. Dad's hoots and sighs, with an occasional swear word, was ingrained in the history of one's memories.

▢▢▢▢

Winter's first snow fall, even if it never survives when it hits the ground, it was considered the first snow fall of the winter. Neighborhood kids dug deep into storage areas, garages and attics until hockey sticks and the odd pad was found. Quickly groups gathered at any point on Roosevelt Street to challenge themselves to a game of street hockey. Everyone showed up be he young, old, big or small. Street hockey was for everyone.

Jerry, Tom and Pat, Francis and Terry, Walter, Billy, Richard, Mark, Bart, the McFarling boys, even the odd strange kid would show up. As important as street hockey is it was unorganized but organized by ingrained rules. No one had to say lets get started. Everyone tossed their sticks into a pile then someone kneeled down, shuffled the sticks, with closed eyes began tossing a stick right then left. Voila, those were the teams. No one complained and no one played positions. Unorganized organized hockey was played and enjoyed.

That first street hockey game of the season was rough on hockey sticks. Soon the anticipated fall of snow came. Frayed sticks were taped up with sticky black electrical tape. Games came and went as the snow piled higher and higher. With snow packed on the street, hockey was at it's finest. Kids slipped and slid, ran and checked each other into the ten foot high snow banks. There were no fancy hockey nets with webbing. Two snow piles set at a stick's length apart were the goal posts. In the crease the goalie was goal keeper and referee. He and he alone declared if he had been scored upon.

"No goal!" Billy 'Gump' Wozny stated matter of fact. "The ball is under my leg."

Sure enough Billy had stopped the shot spread eagle style. Under his goalie pad, that seemed as large as he was short, the faded tennis ball was wedged between leg and pad.

"Face off." called out Tom.

Quickly everyone returned to their own side for the face off. Tom dropped the ball between himself and Jerry. After a small bounce Jerry took possession and carried the ball towards Billy. Kids swarmed like honey bees of summer. In came Richard stick handling as if he had turned pro. Jerry dodged using his eyes to entice Richard to follow in the wrong direction. Terry was fast on the left wing slipping by on thread-less boots.

This past summer Jerry and Richard had become friends doing kid things together. Just because you are on opposite sides in a road hockey game does not mean friends are rivals. With a quick pass Jerry gave Walter a lead to the goal. Billy began to crouch behind his goalie pads.

In remembering the past summer Jerry was a couple of years older than Richard but not much bigger. With a growth spurt and

Mother's good cooking Richard had gained a few pounds. Though skinny and lanky he had made an unknowing effort gaining in size.

A good clean pass and Jerry figured to finish off his move with a body check. To make a good check on his buddy Richard was the plan. With shoulder lowered Jerry made his move. As surprised as anyone was Richard when Jerry seemed to bounce off and crash onto the snow packed road.

"He shoots, he scores." rejoiced Walter after his shot squeezed past Billy.

Billy nodded conformation. "It was hit-off of my shoulder." Behind his pads, Billy lumbered to stand, but when a shot was flying towards his net he was slick and quick.

After picking himself up Jerry wearyingly gave a stare towards Richard who innocently shrugged off the incident. In some respects it is funny in how the mind of a child works. What extremes a child will take in a game when someone younger accomplishes success beyond his abilities. Out on the road in this street hockey game the kids pretended they were famous hockey stars. Like their heroes, they are expected not to fail.

Maurice 'Rocket' Richard in his hay day of professional hockey was not known for being a gentleman on the ice. In a game of brawn and finesse Richard dealt out as much abuse as he received. Checks clean or dirty counted towards the quest for Stanley's trophy of excellence.

Billy the Gump stopped another slap shot from twenty feet away. Legs split and hands scrambled for the bouncing ball. Kids with their hockey heroes in their minds and voices called out their own plays.

"Gordie Howe winds up . . . and slaps a sizzle`er."

"It is wide . . . behind the net Makita picks up the loose puck . . . it is a long pass to Hull . . . he misses."

"Sawchuck fans . . . regains the loose puck . . . another slap shot."

Street hockey knows no boundaries of teams and arenas. Any famous player can play with any other famous player on Roosevelt Street.

"A loose puck . . . Rocket Richard picks it up and carries it down the left side of the ice." Richard almost had a breakaway.

In the heat of a fast paced game, tempers flared. Sometimes the reality of a friendly game is forgotten. Had Jerry, Richard's summer time friend turned mean? Had he forgotten that this was just a game. To everyone who observed the play would attest that Jerry's move was dirty hockey. Obviously dirty tricks and bad sportsmanship were watched by fans on television. Hockey was not censored, how could it be? Not everyone that watched hockey played dirty, but some did.

"Rocket Richard has the puck . . . a clear breakaway down the side of the rink." Richard noticed Jerry crossing the road with the intent to check him into the snowbank. "The Rocket fakes, tries a spin into the centre of the ice."

Not a clean check by anyone's standards Jerry shoved his stick between Richard's legs and lifted the blade. Knowing enough about the tenderness of his family jewels Richard pressed his knees together to prevent injury. On the same motion Jerry pushed his bulk into his friend sending him hard to the road ice not the softness of the snow bank.

In an instant the game had stopped. No one chased the ball. As if everyone was standing frozen in time just watched and waited for Richard's reaction to the check. The Rocket would never leave a check like that, go unanswered. Without giving the matter an inclination or regard Richard dropped his stick, stood and lunged towards Jerry.

"Fight . . . , fight . . . time out." echoed Terry's voice through the bitter cold air.

"Get him."

"Knock him down."

"You can take him." encouraged Mark, Richard's best friend when growing up.

After Richard moved down the street to his new home, a bit of the childhood friendship faded. Friends no matter what, are still kindred best friends.

"Come on Richard you can take him."

Though Jerry was a couple of years older and street wise Richard had gained height and untested growing strength. Jerry dropped his stick and faced up to Richard with several pushes.

"Make room." Francis and Tom organized a circle of rites. "Give them space to fight."

"Do not let him take you Jerry." yelled out an older kid with a taste of hate in his voice. "He is just a wimp that cannot take a check."

A circle of rites? In a circle surrounded by kids that one play's with. Here and now they were the spectators and the judges of the fight's outcome. Put up a good fight and they would pat you on the back . Show signs of weakness and at every opportunity they would check you as hard as they could.

Jerry felt a bit caught off guard, he miss-judged Richard's mass. Fighting off Richard's attempts to grab his coat Jerry pushed back harder. Arms struggled and grabbed and pushed back and forth.

"You got him now." confirmed a confident best friend. "You got him good."

Cold hard road ice, smacked against Jerry's back. Now with the upper hand Richard had Jerry pinned to the road. Eyes locked in on each other. Fear showed in one set of greenish eyes and dominance in a set of dark brown eyes.

"Punch him . . . this is hockey . . . you have to throw punches." informed Billy from the circle of provoking voices. "Punch his lights out."

Locked arms tried to push up into Richard's chest. He had Jerry pined with the weight of his legs on Jerry's arms. Both of Richard's arms were free able to strike the blows all were yelling to see. A clear angle was available to land a punch to Jerry's eye. With a mighty blow Jerry's eye was sure to be black and blue. The guys would be patting Richard on the back for a well fought street hockey fight.

"Now . . . get him . . . give him a good one in the eye." demanded Francis, holding back the boys with outstretched arms. "We cannot start the game until this fight is over."

Both Jerry and Richard heard the voices as their struggle for control continued. No doubt each was thinking of what the other was thinking. All summer they had been friends with sleep-outs in the tent, raiding gardens, hunting and fighting mud-fights side by side. Thoughts all came back to the present, a hockey game, a dirty check and the bystander's view of a fight.

Rubber boots squeaked against the road ice. On this morning there had not been many cars passing threatening to break up the fight. Kids dressed in wool winter coats, toques, leather mitts and Stanfields' maritime-made long underwear, relished in Canadian winters and Canadian hockey.

Hockey the game of strategy, talent, the Stanley Cup and hand-shakes at the end of a game. Gentlemen of

Sportsmanship fist fighting instead of playing the great sport.

"You got me pinned down." said Jerry to Richard through puffs of cold air with a weak voice. "If you are going to hit me then hit me."

Words of encouragement from Jerry, was not what Richard had expected. Richard had a clenched fist inside of a bulky leather mitt. At any moment a black eye blow could be delivered.

"If you are going to fight, fight!" anger was in Jerry's voice as if he was getting angry because he was not getting punched.

"Get him."

"What are you doing?"

"Punch his lights out."

Through the voices of encouragement Richard stood straight up over Jerry. Below his friend lay breathing heavy beneath spread legs. Huge, tall and massive felt Richard, he felt bigger than the biggest kid around. Did Jerry sense anything, was he humiliated?

"What! Are you . . . crazy, you had him beat?" complained Bart after wiping a dripping nose on the back of his mitt. "You could have ploughed him."

An alien cold sweat swept through Richard's body. Into each one of the guy's eyes Richard looked. The return look was of disrespect. A hockey code and the circle of rites had been broken.

"Some fight!"

"A waste of time."

"Let's play hockey." announced Pat as the circle broke up. "Same teams."

More of the kids stood by Jerry talking all at one time. Those words were gibberish to Richard who stood cast to the side.

"Here is your stick Richard." Mark said, patting him righteously on the back. "You did okay. Do not let this incident bother you."

For a moment, Richard stood there watching the boys continue calling out the game and playing as if they were hockey's heroes. Feeling rejected Richard crossed the intersection of Balfour and Roosevelt Streets and headed home.

Many a street hockey game was played that winter and countless winters after. The same kids played the game. Older kids left when they discovered girls. Younger brothers stepped in when they were able to hold a stick and run.

In a day, the fight was forgotten, Richard played the next game. No one seemed to care, everything that happened was yesterday's news. Jerry and Richard still raided gardens and slept out in the tent during the summers in the back yards. When it came to hockey though Jerry bumped but never dirty checked Richard. Something inside of Richard said it was okay to resist a check with equal or harder resistance. Richard never went out of his way to instigate a check.

HOT SUMMERS
CHAPTER 14
TIRE SWING

Most memories, that are made and remembered, seem to happen during the summer months. Sure there are events worth remembering during school but what kid wants to brag about grades, pictures drawn and a good attendance ribbon.

It is the freedom of summer that is most memorable. No morning ritual of waking then standing in line at the bathroom door. Shoveling down oatmeal, no, oatmeal should be savoured with a toping of brown sugar and cooled with cream. On school days there is no time to savor, it is rush, rush, rush, down your food, get dressed and march out of the door. Mothers take a nap on the couch while their kids reluctantly trudge off to school anticipating recess.

Roosevelt Street was deserted, there was not a kid in sight. No one was playing ball in the back yards. Even the girls had disappeared. Richard had made the rounds weaving his way from back yards to favorite fields, secret spots and back to his starting position.

Contemplating the demise of neighborhood kids, Richard sat down on the twisted green front porch. His new house on the corner of Balfour and Roosevelt Streets was now comfortable. It was as if he had lived there all of his life. Even when he walked by the old two story house that he had spent five years in seemed foreign. In his child's memory he could not remember much about the inside of the house. People only seem to recall memories when they are older and have time to sit and recall past experiences.

There on the green wooden porch with his chin resting on his hands Richard watched nothing going by on the street. For a kid of twelve years this moment of reflection was of no fun.

Two tall silver poplar trees with limbs burdened with leaves shaded the front yard and the porch. Richard sat cool and relaxed in a dream state when his beat friend Mark came walking southward on the street.

Mark stood on the road looking at Richard. Mark's reddish brown hair and freckles were brightened under the summer sun. A summer attire for Mark was an off coloured tee-shirt, shorts and black canvas running shoes on feet without socks.

"What is the matter Richard, how come you are sitting there doing nothing?" Words broke the silence of contemplation. "Are you grounded or something?"

"Hey Mark, no I ain't grounded." Richard lifted his head from his hands but stayed sitting. "There just ain't no one around to play with. I cannot find anyone."

Mark pointed down the road towards the south end of Roosevelt Street. A towel hung from his hand. "Everyone is at the creek. There is a tire on a rope to swing out over the creek."

Richard leaned as if he were able to see to the end of the street. "And anyone can go and use it?"

"Yeah, everyone is there now." Mark grabbed at his clothes. "I had to go home and get other clothes. I fell in and got wet." Holding out his towel Mark presented it to Richard. "I am ready now just in case, I fall and get wet again."

Standing up with anticipation, Richard waited for Mark's invitation. "Everyone gets to take a turn?"

"Sure." said Mark beckoning with an arm for Richard to follow him. "Come on let's go."

That was all that was needed to entice a kid, a simple invitation. There was no need to leave a message or tell anyone where a kid was off to. Kids lived the life of kids just like the Little Rascals just going and doing what kids do best.

□□□□

At this historical time in the early sixties kids still created their own fun, innocent fun. No one was out to hurt another kid, no one was going to beat up another kid. This was Roosevelt Street far from the turmoil of a big city, far removed from the building tensions and conflicts of the American's Vietnam engagement.

This was Canada. Though television brought the conflicts to inquisitive eyes, it was foreign not happening on one's door step. Violence came one night to the television screens of the people world wide. Impressions that linger etched in a child's mind.

In the comfort of home Richard sat with his Mom and Dad watching the news of the world on television. Without warning live coverage from Vietnam filled the once make-believe image he had of television. A man pointed a pistol to the temple of another man who had his hands bound by rope. There was only a puff of gun powder smoke. A memory of life passed within a moment. Suddenly a gush of blood spurted from the man's temple before he collapsed to the ground. This was the images of war a world away brought before the eyes of everyone on television screens. Life continues for everyone else. Richard seemed to accept the fact that evil happens elsewhere.

☐☐☐☐

Today it would be Mark taking him to the creek to experience the thrill of hanging onto a tire and riding a rope out over a cold flowing creek.

At the end of Roosevelt Street, a creek crossed its path. Spanning the creek, a grey painted steel foot bridge lead from one side to the other. The south side of the street was a very short section. Following on Mark's heels Richard entered the woods along the side of the creek. Yelps and screams echoed from within the confines of the bush.

In an opening cleared on the bank of the creek all of the neighborhood kids had gathered. McFarlings, McAuleys, Heberts, Mckenzies and Thibodeau kids were there. Older teenagers, boys, girls, younger brothers and sisters enjoying a childhood pastime. Some were enjoying an adult pastime.

Leaning out over the creek's bank a large hardwood tree extended a limb out over the water. Tied securely to the limb a heavy hemp rope looped around a skinny discarded tire.

Skinny Laura had ran and jumped out over the water swinging back to the bank on the tire swing. Dave, an advanced teenager, jumped up taking the tire swing with both hands leaned far back then ran and leaped. He was high and it looked as if he was out over the other side of the creek. At the peek of his ride Dave let go and seemed to hang in mid air before splashing into the cold creek. Clambering up the bank Dave shook off the water then sat on a blanket he shared with a girl. Dave and his female friend began to smooch.

Mark whispered to Richard. "They are making out."

"When do we get out turn?" asked Richard, he scanned the area and the group of kids.

Mark turned with a bewildered look then realized that Richard was concerned about a turn on the tire swing. "Just wait for an opening then take a turn."

Laughter and antics on the tire swing were as good as any big time circus. Kids swung by feet and legs or sitting inside of the tire. Bigger kids tested their strength by hanging by one hand. Some made it, others ended up in the drink.

From observing the many swings, it occurred to Richard that the object of the game was to swing out and around the tree without falling off. Surely if a skinny girl like Laura could do it so could Richard, but Mark fell into the water.

Richard watched Laura swing out then back. "Hi Richard." said Laura. "Are you going to try the swing?" she asked jumping from the swing and landing next to Richard.

Mark grabbed the tire and ran then flung himself out over the water.

"I can do that." said Richard, with as much confidence as he could muster in front of Laura. "Yeah I am going to try it." In his mind Richard said to himself that he had to do it. Knowing that he could not swim if he fell into the water he told himself that he had to hang on with all of his might. "As soon as I get a turn."

Laura, being mostly skin and bones with dirty blonde hair, was not shy. Pushing her way in front of older kids she grabbed the loose tire swing. Mark had made the swing out over the creek but his landing was a little short. Laura held the tire as Mark clawed his way up the bank to solid ground.

"Almost fell in." announced Mark Proudly. "I need a bigger run next time."

Some kids nodded, others gave pointers. Most of the pointers came from older kids like Jerry, Tom or Dave.

"You have to leap right when you get to the edge." Jerry planted his foot at the right spot. Others nodded with agreement.

"Here Richard." Laura pushed the tire towards Richard. "Take a turn and run hard."

In front of a girl no boy would back down. Richard had paid attention to the other riders and listened to Jerry's suggestions. Fear, what fear? Could anyone see fear in Richard's eyes? Fear is what gets a mind and body ready for life.

"Watch." Laura took a good hold of the tire and swung out over the creek with her skinny legs kicking at the air. "See, just do it like me."

Helping with the landing, Richard took hold of the tire. "I think I know how." Backing up as far as possible for maximum momentum Richard kept a steady eye for the takeoff point. Jerry's foot print was there in the sand. Fear made him tightly grip the lips of the tire. Feet that were unsure of themselves took solid strides towards the bank's edge, towards the takeoff point.

What was out there over the creek that made kids swing out from firm earth to dangle suspended for a moment? A missed step, a slipping hand and it would be a free fall into cold water that would shiver a kid despite the heat of the day. A stimulation to make a kid sense feeling alive. To conquer fear? Fun?

From deep inside of his stomach a weight rose, Richard could feel his insides moving, floating freely. He could see nothing between his feet and the water. The sky moved in 3D through the leaves of the trees. On shore the other kids were blurs of images, their voices a jumble of incoherent words.

'I am flying.' thought Richard. In the thoughts of his mind everything was happening at one time. Not long enough was the ride, it ended before all the emotions of the thrill could be tallied.

No sooner than his feet touched the bank and a butt slid into the root filled earth another kid took a turn, he was questing for the same utopia.

'What a sensation, I have to get another turn.' Richard stood there thinking, his body seemed normal but inside sparks tingled every nerve towards pleasured excitement.

Others took turns then Dave took hold with one hand and sailed out. As if in stop motion he changed hands for the incoming ride. Dave's skinny frame held tight stomach muscles, arm muscles were well defined. High over the bank he let go landing at the feet of his girlfriend. Only inquisitive eyes watched him kiss and 'make out', as Mark quoted.

After each turn, Mark, Richard, Billy, John and other first time kids, they became better, more confident. Seeking an even higher thrill was the challenge after each new stunt. For some it also was the excitement of dropping from the tire into the water. This was the next challenge of bravery.

Walter arrived later in the afternoon to the creek playground. Walter stood as tall as the other kids his age, a year older than Richard and Mark, a solid kid. On his first attempted try he slipped and fell into the cold water. It was hard to tell if he had done it by mistake or intentionally. Dripping ice cold water, from his Sunday best clothes, Walter climbed the creek bank.

"Walter! Where are you going?" asked a concerned Mark. "Are you hurt?"

"No." replied Walter, his clothes seemed to be twice their normal size. "I have to go home and change into my play clothes."

Richard asked. "Are you going to get into trouble?"

"Hey, Walter." Jerry twitched a twig between his teeth as he talked. "Stay here until your clothes dry."

"No, I better go home."

Another splash occurred, two kids together swung out over the water on the tire swing. Everyone carried on as Walter sloshed along the path towards the road and home.

Time passed slowly while the fun lingered on an endless hot July day. The outside world was a lifetime away. Silence occurred when everyone noticed Walter standing on the path leading to the play area. Hovering like a giant behind Walter stood his Dad. Walter had changed clothes, he seemed okay, it did not look like he had gotten into trouble. Silence prevailed under the scrutiny of an adult's authoritative eye.

"Go ahead continue to play." Walter's Dad's voice echoed with a deep resonance. "I am just here to see if the tire swing is tied securely and if the water is not too deep.

After a moment's thought the kids continued to carry on playing. Dave refrained from making out. Walter took several turns on the swing and never fell into the water. No one noticed Walter's Dad leave. Dave did begin to make out again.

By the lateness of the afternoon Mark and Richard were showing Laura a few tricks on the tire swing. Thrills are thrills, old thrills on a simple tire swing are worth remembering on Roosevelt Street. Dave experienced other kinds of thrills.

HOT SUMMERS
CHAPTER 15
DAM BUILDERS

There was a time when man did not try to turn nature into a fabrication of what man thought nature should be. When a young city grew and expanded new land was developed. Put a road here, a house there, cut trees down then plant new ones. Nature's waterways were not touched. No one filled in a creek or diverted it. When a creek became an obstacle to man, he would build a bridge to cross from side to side.

Fish, birds, cattails, choke-cherry trees all live in or by a creek. No one bothers to put culverts or make a concrete belly for the water to follow. Driving down Second Line towards Brookfield subdivision you would not see today what was there in the past. The creek that flowed across Second Line is but a depression in the earth where water barely trickles through.

One summer, when kids began to venture further and further onto other streets, they began to meet with new kids. Walter, Richard and Jerry were hanging around together this summer when Richard was about twelve and a half years' old. Walter was a year older with Jerry a year more. It had been awhile since Mark and Richard had hung around as best friends. Nothing bad had come between them. Sometimes different interests lead boys in diverse direction. While Mark was vacationing with his family out of town Richard relied on new friends. New friends lead to new and abstract adventures.

Having different friends can be good, sometimes not. Older friends have done and do try new challenges. Richard had not yet reached the speed of his new buddies. Good buddies do not belittle a friend that is a little reluctant or scared to try new temptations. It does take time for one to obtain the ability to face one's own fears. This summer Richard faced some fears and declined a few.

That depression in the earth with a trickle of water was now wide, deep and filled to the brim with water in nineteen-sixty five. Water came from miles and miles away. On days of exploring, with different friends, Richard and company had never found the source. All along the creek there were signs of studious beavers.

Way up somewhere near the beginning of the creek there lived a pair of beavers that must have been great, great, great grandparents by now. When there were too many baby beavers in the house the older ones were told to move out.

On an early spring day a lone beaver swam down the creek to build his new dam and home. Over and over each new eldest beaver born would have to move down the stream. It was no different this spring. On a winding curve on the creek, about a hundred feet from the bridge on Second Line, a beaver decided this location looked like a good place to make a home.

Before the heavy flow of winter's snow melt the bachelor' beaver began to cut the trees for his dam. A beaver builds a good tall strong dam to hold back the water. After that he will set about building a home. It had looked as if the beaver was ahead of schedule on his dam. The snows melt water came, the dam held strong bound together with sticks and mud. From generation to generation the art of dam building was handed down parents to children. This beaver's great, great, great grandparents would have been proud.

It does happen on occasion when nature and civilization collide, disaster is eminent. When in search of more trees, the right size for his home, the beaver ventured close to man's inventions. To every man or animal the grass is always greener on the other side of the fence.

Clouds were sparse, a moon was full. At night the beaver does his best work. So on this night the beaver spotted trees the right size just over the hill. A man-made machine of luxury became an implement of death. Nature met man's society, man killed a creature of nature.

No other beaver mourned his death. Left as a reminder, to its talent, a dam withstood winter's melt water. When the spring rains were over and the dryness of summer came there was a toil taken upon the dam. There was not a beaver to take care of its upkeep. Little by little the water had seeped through weakening the structure. Slowly the water depth began to subside.

Summer is a time when lazy days and sweltering temperatures entice boys and girls to seek cool waters. Several kids from a street east of Roosevelt Street on Whitney Avenue were meandering about the neighborhood. It was Edward and his brother Bill that first noticed the small pool of water behind the weathered beaver dam. A water hole to cool off in on a hot summer day, they could not resist. It was a matter of minutes before the summer tanned kids had discarded shirts, shoes and socks.

Wading knee-deep into the pool was as refreshing as an orange popsicle in ninety degree temperatures. Both Bill and Edward lounged in the refreshing waters. Soon they were splashing then jumping from the creek bank like cannon balls. When Edward, huge for his size, did a cannon ball fifty percent of the water was displaced.

Over the weak section of the beaver dam the water flowed bit by bit eating at the structure. Water from the upper end soon replaced the lost water in the pool. For two playful kids the pool did not fill up fast enough.

With his butt sitting on the sandy bottom and Bill swimming like a beaver around him, Edward stared at the beaver dam. It was as if he had just learned to add two and two together. In Edward's mind the instincts of dam building must have crossed over from the beaver's mind.

There was no need to tell Bill what he was about to do. An eleven-year-old like Bill just imitated his thirteen-year-old brother. To untrained eyes those that noticed the two brothers would have thought they were incarnated beavers. Sticks, logs, stumps with anything that they could get their hands onto was stuffed into the dam. With hands digging deep into the sand bottom of the pool clumps of clay was extracted then pasted to the tangle of sticks.

Both boys acted like eager beavers until the late afternoon told them that they had missed supper. Each day saw them at their new location of entertainment. There were no malls to hang out in, no gangs standing around doing nothing. They were participating in life, enjoying nature. Kids of today cannot enjoy nature unless they have the comfort of home and a mall to visit.

Soon the boy's wading pool got deeper and deeper. By word of mouth it became a crowded watering hole. Family, friends then new friends from the surrounding streets. The logic was, that if there were more kids, the dam had to be bigger. Big Edward, a head and shoulder taller than the others his age, stood up to his neck in the water behind the dam.

Bathing suits and old running shoes were the normal attire for swimming. Edward and Bill sported water goggles. Towels hung scattered on alder branches. People passing by stopped on the bridge to watch with happy amusement. Jerry had heard from a friend and joined the swimmers. In turn he told his sisters and Walter and Richard.

This new water spa had to be checked out. Jerry, Walter and Richard headed to the dam. Jerry did not hesitate, he soaked playfully in the water. Being water likable is not for everyone, Richard held back. Was it a matter of being cautious or down right scared of the unknown beneath the water's surface? Being unable to see the bottom or touch the bottom is something of a puzzle, Richard saw it this way.

One can still stand by enjoying others play and be as satisfied. An old steel wire farm fence divided the road from the dam. Unsupported wire crossed the known rough water before it went under the bridge. Sitting or leaning on the fence was where Richard enjoyed passing the time watching others entertain.

Before Walter took the plunge into the waiting water, he rushed home to get his Dad's permission. A short while later father and son came to the swimming hole. Dad stood leaning against the fence eyeing the kids, pool, dam and the merriment. With a nod given Walter cannon balled into the water. Richard and Walter's Dad leaned silently watching, watching was fun.

No matter how much fun, fun is, some people cannot or will not leave things as they were. Days later city workers dismantled the dam. Face's of disappointment, on the gathered kids prevented from enjoying their enjoyment, is sad. There are those that relish in preventing the spread of happiness. Those same people today are known to want to prevent kids from hanging around doing nothing. Who forced them into doing nothing? These same people that prevent others from enjoying simple pleasures are the root of the problem.

Days after the dam was removed, the flow of water had increased. Other real beaver dams further up the creek had been destroyed. Man was now trying to control nature. They could not or would not let nature be. Richard passed across the bridge, stopped and watched the fast-moving water rush over boulders beneath the bridge. The old farm fence crossing the creek was barely two feet above the foaming water.

Thinking things out then trying to confront and tame his fears, was Richard's method. Swimming in the creek was out of the question. It was now September where temperatures change and swimming is next summer's challenge. This creek still could be challenged. After the decision was made Richard climbed down the embankment to the creek's edge. Rushing water's roar filled his ears. Lost were the sounds of vehicles on Second Line, lost were the sounds from the forest.

Once a mind is committed, the body follows. Placing a foot in the square wire openings one after another, hands and proper leaning was all that was required to cross the creek. They say not to look down if fear, fears you. Conquering fear means looking down into the turbulent waters.

There was no one on the bridge watching, no kids at the broken dam, no one waiting when Richard climbed down off of the fence. Who needs a witnessing audience? Gratification was self pride in a kid's mind when his fear was conquered. How proud Richard walked with firm steps down the length of Roosevelt Street on his way home.

HOT SUMMERS
CHAPTER 16
RIVER RAFT

Before people became paranoid about, . . . just about everything. Before fences, boundaries, rules and limitations there was a world to discover. At the south end of Roosevelt Street across the foot bridge and Wallace Terrace was a bush. Most of the land was now second growth bushes with small shrubs, small trees and tall grass. It was in this new area that the boys from Roosevelt Street sought to explore.

Most of the land was owned by Algoma Steel, a steel mill that in a way supported the growth of a Sault Ste. Marie and the surrounding Township. All of the land, located south of Wallace Terrace to the main mill then west about five miles including the shore line along St. Mary's river, was Algoma Steel property.

On a day out exploring the boys did not know or care about the ownership of the land. There were no fences or guards to chase them away. It was just land keeping them away from reaching the river. Yes the river where Tom and Pat had found a small bay with an Island in it.

No one can keep a good-thing a secret. It was Tom and Pat who invited Jerry, Richard and Walter to come and explore their south sea type of island.

"You will not believe it." piped up a blonde haired Tom.

"Yeah it is great." added Pat who resembled his brother.

In some families, mannerisms, features and voice are all the same within the kids. Tom and Pat and their three younger brothers all resembled each other. Blue eyes or shades of blue green, blonde hair cut short on the sides and left longer on the top, was their presence. They even dressed alike. Like all families clothes were always hand-me-downs. That was a fact of life.

Jerry questioned the brother. "Where is this place?"

"Through the bush at the end of the street." Tom pointed in a southerly direction.

"Do you want to join us?"

"Sure Pat." answered Richard for Jerry and Walter.

Walter seemed excited at the moment then said. "I will have to ask my dad first."

Everyone looked at Walter without saying anything. There was a pause of silence until Walter added. "He will say yes. I just need to let him know where I am going."

"Are you going to go now?"

"Not now Richard." Pat answered, he pulled the strap of his canteen onto his shoulder. "We just came back from there. But first thing tomorrow morning we are going back."

Tom gave a few orders, he was the unofficial leader. Tom was the one that knew the way. "Bring a lunch, a coat, a knife and be ready at eight o'clock in the morning."

"Where do we meet?" asked a concerned Walter. In his mind he was not sure if his dad would let him go with the guys.

Tom pointed to Jerry first. "We will get Jerry first, he lives next door to us, then pickup Richard then Walter."

Nodding heads confirmed the arrangement.

"If you ain't ready, we will not wait."

It was only four o'clock in the afternoon but everyone scattered off home. A new adventure was waiting, anticipating tomorrow's excursion. Plans had to be thought of, gear needed to be gathered.

Over the past week, Tom and Pat had made countless trips back and forth to their secret island. Bits of this and that, tools and essentials that they required were stashed somewhere near the bay.

Jerry was use to the outdoors, he had a good pocket knife, a small axe and a green canvas packsack. That packsack was a hand-me-down from his father, war surpluses. Into that sack Jerry stuffed everything, knives, fork, band-aid and even a cup and a pot.

"Dad, do you think I could go with Tom, Pat, Jerry and Richard?" Walter interrupted his Dad's supper. "They are all going hiking to a bay over there by the river, all day exploring." said Walter between short breaths. "Would it be all right if I go with them?"

Supper continued as his dad thought the idea through. Dad's thorough questions were asked and important advice with wilderness pointers given. Walter had received permission. Late that night Walter's Mom made him a good lunch of sandwiches, an apple, an orange and fresh cookies all wrapped nicely and packed into a brown paper bag. Before bedtime Walter's dad lent him his pocket knife to use.

Richard was not a night person, he was an early morning riser. That night before the outing he headed to bed early. He did not want to miss the guys in the morning. There in his basement bedroom laying in bed Richard looked out of the small window. Clouds had moved in, the sky darkened as rain threatened to fall. As Richard worried about the next day being ruined, the pitter-patter of rain drops lulled him to sleep.

Before the morning light gave its heat of the life Richard was up getting ready for the outing. In the silence of the house as his brothers, sister and parents slept Richard began making a lunch. From the utensil drawer he selected a paring knife then rapped it in cardboard. With peanut butter and strawberry sandwiches, an apple and oat meal cookies they were loosely placed in a bread bag along with the knife. Checking his inventory, lunch, knife, running shoes, coat and toilet paper stuffed into a back pocket Richard decided that he was ready. Ready he was as he sat waiting on the front porch with the sun inching its way into the sky. Being an hour early was about right for Richard.

Loaded down with rope and an axe Tom, Pat and Jerry made their way down the road. There was no time to stop to talk. Rushing to the road Richard joined the troupe. Walter joined as the boys paraded past his house.

"If you have forgotten something. " informed Tom. "Then it is too bad."

Off went the boys down the road, across the foot bridge, across Wallace Terrace and into the bush. Tom was leading the way because he knew where the hidden entrance to the path was. Last night's hint of foul weather only left damp ground that soon would evaporate under a hot summer day. Humid heat rose from the ground. Soon coats would be removed as tee-shirts clung to sticky bodies.

To those following Tom and Pat it felt like the walking was lasting forever. Bushes were all around, even the sky was hidden by the abundance of large leafed trees. It was almost like kids in the back seat of an automobile on a family trip when someone asks. 'Are we almost there yet?'

Tom assured the doubtful. "Almost there." said for the fifth time.

Finally the trail ended at the sandy shore of a small bay. A light fog hovered in the distance over the water. There in the middle of the bay an island sat as if suspended in mid air. Silence prevailed over the scene. Not a bird's sound, not a ripple on the light blue water. As close to Shangri-La as it was going to get in Northern Ontario.

The great St. Mary's River, not a river in the sense of a river, more like a channel that delivers the excess water from Lake Superior. From the largest of the great lakes water flows through the St. Mary's River to Lake Huron some twenty miles away.

Native Canadians gathered at White Fish Island in the middle of Ste. Mary's River to fish for whitefish. Always a meeting place for the Ojibway Native Canadians for over three hundred tears before a single white man had arrived.

Here on the same shore the boys ventured without knowledge or reverence for past history. True to real explorers each step they took was a new adventure of discovery. New to them as if they were the first to set a foot on virgin land. Upon seeing the small island they had experienced the same sensations that the first explores must have felt.

While the other boys discussed the trail, equipment, the depth of water Richard just took in the picturesque view. Like breathing in the breath of life he soaked up his surroundings to recall at future reminiscing moments.

Jerry broke Richard's moment of silence. "I bet you I can make a rock float."

"No way." replied Richard. "Rocks are too heavy to float."

Jerry picked up a rock that looked to weigh two or three pounds. It looked like someone had drilled hundreds of little holes all over the rock. Jerry strained to lift it from its resting spot then moved to place it in the water. Richard bent over to make sure the rock was not touching bottom. Sure enough the rock was floating.

Eyes were wide, Richard poked at the rock, it bobbed in the water. "Unreal, how is it able to float?"

"Pick it up." encouraged Jerry.

Bending his knees in anticipation of lifting a heavy weight Richard reached for the odd shaped rock. Surprisingly the rock was not heavy as Jerry pretended it to be. It felt as light as feathers. Richard excitedly picked up several other rocks and placed them in the water. They floated easily as they bobbed in the light waves from the legs of the boys making their way out towards the island.

Floating rocks were not real rocks, they only looked like rocks. Their creator was the steel mill. After steel is made, a by-product is produced and discarded. Sulfide bonded with oxygen and other evaporating gases when cooled leaves a puck-marked slag deposit. Slag was light enough to float. Mounds of slag filled land lay west of the steel mill. A waste that now blackens the shoreline.

"Are you guys coming?" asked Pat of the lagging boys.

It was Jerry and Richard pulling up the rear. Before following the other boys towards the island Richard added a few more rocks to the water. Shallow water that was only a knee deep was as warm as bath tub water. Summer's warm days heated the earth and the shallow water.

With gear on their shoulders, lunches kept dry, the boys walked in single-file up the shore of the island. They were there, now what where Tom and Pat up to, what was all the gear for?

"Okay Tom." was Walter's demanded as he wrung out the water from his pant legs. "What is the secret project?"

"Right there." Tom said with bold pride. "A raft."

Several logs had been laid out side by side. Other green logs lay near by ready to be latched together to form a skeletal raft. The makings of a solid raft where at hand. Today was the day Tom and Pat had planed to finish making it and launching it into the river.

Walter looked the logs over at the way they were arranged and how they were fastened together. "Do you guys know how to build a raft?"

Standing tall with hands on his hips, Tom looked down upon his raft. "Yeah, I think so."

Pat backed brother Tom up. "We, . . . sure do!"

Logs float, everyone knows that. Well some trees float better than others. Loggers use to run logs down rivers all the time. If the difference in types of trees and the float ability was known by Tom and Pat, maybe they would have been more sure of their reply to Walter.

Jerry and Richard tried to lift a cut log. Their straining with grunts and groans was more impressive then the distance the log was moved. It was obvious, no one said anything, but this log would be one to float at little under the surface of the water. It was Tom and Pat's raft and their plan to sail her. In all cases of ship building there are workers needed for the work, thus the assistance of Walter, Richard and Jerry.

"We need more logs for the raft." Tom interrupted Jerry and Richard's rest. "You two, help put the logs in place, Pat, you tie up the logs."

Tom was beginning to sound like a captain Hook. Luckily they were on land, it would be easier to desert.

"Walter and I will cut more trees down and haul them here." said Tom anxiously, the day was wearing on.

For young boys, giving free labour with no rewards foreseeable, their sweat began building under the cool fog. By late morning the fog had dispersed under the sun's rays. At midday the river seemed calm. A mile across the river, the shores of the American side looked peaceful and green. Only the sounds of the odd jet taking off or landing from the distance broke the stillness of the day. On a hill there could be seen the rotating radar on the American army base. To the boys it was just a fixture on the horizon. Maybe the Americans were involved in the Viet Nam war but Canada and the boys carried on living life without hostilities.

Once the fog had lifted the loud fog horns that had sounded earlier could now be placed to corresponding lake- freighters. Thousand-foot Lakers full and empty passed up and down the river. Cargos of iron ore, fuel oil and wheat from the lake-head passed through the busiest locks in the world. Some inland ships were bigger than ocean vessels. Today Tom and Pat hoped to ply the same waters alongside of those behemoths.

Without Tom's okay the boy's stomachs decided it was time for lunch. Eagerly they reached into their lunch sacks to retrieve a variety of sandwiches, cookies and fruit. Fresh water from a clean river quenched their thirst.

Tom joined the boys sitting on the logs of the raft. There was not much of a lunch left in the lunch bag to be shared by Tom and his brother. Pat had been hungry and took the liberty of eating a bit of Tom's allotted share.

In the style of Tom Sawyer, Tom reeled a yarn of setting sail with their raft. Floating down the river passing Lakers and visiting whatever was around the bend intrigued Tom and Pat and their listeners. Tom dreamed of experiencing the events that he had read about. He wanted to be the character of make-believe in the Tom Sawyer stories.

Tom had everyone inspired. All were ready to sign on as deck hands. To have the gift to just do whatever is in one's mind is wonderful. Not everyone is willing to do something without knowing the consequences of their actions. A true great explorer just does, they live each day and each step as it occurs willingly accepting whatever happens.

Tom stood stretching back to look at the sun in the sky. "Let's hurry and get this raft finished."

After being inspired by Tom's tales the boys jumped up eager to work. All of the logs that were needed were lined up. Pat tied the last of the rope around, up and over the logs. Cross poles held the ends of the raft together.

On the little island water slapped at the sand shore with lapping waves. By mid afternoon the wind from the north-west began blowing straight down the length of the river. The once calm river now held two to three foot waves. No one paid attention to little details such as weather.

"Push!" encouraged Tom.

"I am, I am." grunted Walter, his forehead showing the sweat of his labour.

With Tom and Walter lifting on poles the other three pushed and pulled the heavy logs into the water.

"Almost there." That same line Tom said over again. He had said that they were on the right path. "Almost there." Meant that there was still a long way to go. "Almost there."

Rocks were moved, logs were put under the raft. What- ever it took was used to try and move the raft inches closer to free floating in the water.

"Almost there." Tom again assured the boys.

On a final heave-ho from over strained young bodies the raft slipped into the water. The boys yelled back to Tom. "Almost there." Their laughter meant to make fun of Tom.

Tom and Pat jumped onto the raft with their push poles. Just their added weight sank the raft onto the sand below the water surface. Over the dense logs the river-water washed cold water.

"Are you coming? Who is coming?" asked Tom, leaning on the push pole forcing the raft out into deeper water.

Richard was no sailor, he declined. Jerry and Walter debated the added weight to the submerging raft, they respectfully declined. Tom and Pat seemed to have no fear. From the shore the boys watched the raft slowly bobbing its way deeper into the flow of the river. Soon their friends looked featureless while the in-between distance increased. White caps of foam crested with each wave.

"Well, they are on their adventure." Jerry confirmed what Walter and Richard knew. "No use for us to stay here."

Walter and Richard nodded. With agreement they collected their belongings and crossed back over the island to the bay side. By late afternoon the water depth had increased. In some sections the water reached to their thighs. No longer was the water pee warm. A boy's manhood shriveled under the cold water conditions. Slag rocks bobbed in the waves of the bay while the boys entered the trail towards home.

Adventures are great no matter what part of the adventure one plays in it. Tom and Pat had a little more adventure than the rest of the boys. It was their plan to sail down the river, but was it as adventuresome as a good Mark Twain story.

Ships in the main channel towered above the water line. Tom and Pat felt like ants in a bath tub. Cold water lapped over their little raft freezing their feet and toes. Soon the water depth began to swallow the length of their push poles. Their adventure of floating down the river was not anything like Mark Twain's story of a lazy Mississippi River. With disappointment Tom and Pat pushed towards the rocky shore of the St. Mary's river.

Boulders on shore locked the raft into its clutches. Tom and Pat abandoned the raft and made their way over the rocks to the safety of solid ground. A long walk, along the shoreline back to the trail and home, would be the time allotted for reflection upon their adventure. A failure? No, any adventure taken is a success. Being well, is a good state to be in. On the rocky shores of the St. Mary's river the raft was not as lucky. Rough waves beat the raft against the rocks until individual logs broke away washing up in a line on the river bank.

Most adventures, that happen to kids in life, are all less than spectacular. Only in later years of retelling stories do they become larger than life. Each individual recalls the story differently. It would be interesting to hear each version of the story by the kid that was there. Each kid on Roosevelt Street has a different version of stories to tell. Each version is true. Stories told are always interesting to read and listen to.

FORTS
CHAPTER 17
SNOW FORT

Remember that winter! Everyone has a winter to remember. It lasted the longest, it was the coldest. It was the winter where the snow started in mid October and never stopped until spring. Snow banks were mountains hiding the houses from the road. North-west winds brought the cold. From morning through the night blowing snow swirled belting hard against frosted glass. The next morning snow drifts crossed driveways, banked up against houses and buried bushes and trees.

On blustery winters is when the hearty souls of the youth venture out. It was the kind of winter Richard loved. Most of the neighborhood kids stayed inside, they had better things to do, or they were getting soft. Sure there were the odd road hockey games and king of the hill fights. Every driveway had a mountain of snow that needed to be conquered. Boys of ten, eleven, even up to fourteen climbed their way to the top to defend their driveway mountain. Onto the next driveway, a new hill and a new chance to be declared the king of the hill.

Under the street lights, that were fairly new to the street, Mark, Richard and Jerry began digging into the snow bank at the end of their driveways. A walled conclave that gave shelter from passing vehicles. With snow balls ready, an attack was launched at passing vehicles.

I guess people assumed that kids were just having fun and were not out to hurt anyone or any vehicle. Snow balls were just soft puffs of millions of snowflakes. Parents were more tolerant in the good ole days. No one really got into serious trouble.

Roads on a good winter always had at lest four inches of hard packed snow. There was never sand or salt spread on the roads. Ploughs did not scrape right down to the gravel of the road.

After the road plough passed by at three-o'clock in the morning the road would start to be packed as cars carried their owners to work. With a weak winter's sun heating the top layer of snow by early evening the road would be ideal for sliding.

Always on the street would be four to six kids out to play, even girls joined in. Billy, Bart, Jerry, Pat, Terry, Richard and others were out to do some sliding. Laura would not let fun pass her by, she could out-do some of the boys her age.

Decoys would line the road. Drivers would slow down knowing that the road was slippery. Then the boys that were hiding in driveways would sneak out as the car passed. Sliding equipment consisted of rubber overshoes that were a year old. Worn out treads were the best for sliding.

Sneaking out, the boys would grab hold of the car's bumper and crouch down. Going the distance meant hanging on for at least three driveways. Sometimes six boys would claim room on one bumper. Feet slipped and slid as boys tried to force each other off. Great riders swung out to the side and hung on with one hand. Walking the bumper meant going from one side to the other without falling off.

Surely the fun was not just for the kids, the drivers would slow down then speed up or fishtail to try and loose hangers. Some drivers were real slow drivers. A beginner could hitch a ride down the length of Roosevelt Street then hitch back on the bumper of another slow driver. Good riders passed those rides up as un-challenging.

In the winter on weekdays a city buss would pass once an hour. That was the big challenge in hitching a ride down three streets, you would have to be good. The buss bumper would be filled by bigger boys out only for the slid behind a buss.

The only down fall recalled would be the guys that wore woolen mitts. Always two or three pairs would be left frozen to bumpers on busses and cars.

As the years advanced roads were salted and sanded. This became a major deterrent to the sliding sport. Great riders can still be remembered, Jerry, Tom, Dave. Kids from other streets came to challenge and show off their tricks of the sport.

☐☐☐☐

This year there was just too much snow to use the roads. Light sparkling snowflakes fell every day. A snow plough would pass by clearing one side at a time. By the time it had passed again on the opposite side the cleared side would be freshly filled.

So what to do with all of this snow? Richard visited his friends one at a time coaxing them out into the blowing storms. For some reason Richard enjoyed storms. When it was cold, blowing with zero visibility that was when Richard enjoyed himself. Odd? If it were the worst storm of the year then the better, he could not wait to pit himself against nature.

Sure the other boys would venture out for a while then some reason forced them to return to the warmth of their homes. At those brief times Richard and whom-ever was enticed would dig out snow forts in the deep snow banks at the ends of driveways. Richard helped Billy start one then Pat and Jerry, Mark was the last. Snow forts were started but were never finished.

One blowing, cold, zero visibility night, the best night to be out in, Richard ventured face first into the whipping snow storm. Waist-deep in snow was a challenge to walk through in back yards. Snow drifts were blowing up against the small blue garage. Richard climbed up onto the peaked roof, standing there, he was able to see gusts of blowing snow whipping around dimly lit house lights. A picture perfect night of shadows, white swirls of wind, black tumbling clouds and billowy soft snow drifts.

With a leap Richard jumped into the wind destined for the snow drift below. Wind pushed snow up the snow drift into Richard's face. The soft snow billowed burying him up to and over his shoulders. It was a soft landing, feet first. Like quicksand the drift of snow swallowed the daredevil jumper.

Hard firm ground had to be beneath his feet, he could not feel the hard ground. For that matter Richard was unable to move his legs. It was lucky that he did not have his arms by his side, for within minutes the blowing snow would have covered him with a smooth angular drift.

Richard stayed there for a minute wallowing in the results of a perfect jump. He in hailed his surroundings with an eye of an artist. People stand for hours looking at a master piece of art. Is not mother nature a work of art, to be admired in her beauty and finesse? With the same care one takes to stop and smell the roses Richard took time to observe the power of a winter storm.

Well it was long enough, snow had begun to pile up under Richard's chin. Like a dog digging for a bone he scooped with his hands shoveling away the snow around his body. When he cleared the snow down to his waist was when legs were able to move. Once out Richard thought of doing the feat of jumping over again. Reason declined the invitation.

Richard had tired of trudging through the deep snow and of attempting another jump from the garage roof. Trying to draw a friend out into this storm would be a wasted effort. Then what to do? Over the past week he had helped others build snow forts, but he did not have one. Well if no one was going to help him, he would help himself.

From the north-west winter's snows and wind blew against the back of the house. Only four feet separated the back corner of the house with the front corner of the garage. It was as if all of the north wind tried to squeeze snow through the narrow opening. Richard stood at the opening looking at the drift of snow taller then he stood.

It was a matter of digging straight into the wall of snow to see how far he could go. Time was of no importance when one 's mind is concentrating on a goal. What Richard's goal was, at the moment, he did not know. Dim light from the bare light bulb on the front eave of the house gave little illumination for his work. Removed snow began to pile up behind him and began to spill over onto the driveway.

Richard helped shovel the driveway, but Dad would not like a pile of snow crowding his station-wagon. After digging a few feet of snow he pushed the snow across the driveway and up onto the snow bank that now hide Walter's house from view.

There were two brothers, Donald and Marc and a baby sister Terri-Lynn in the house. They were sure to be in bed by now. Mom and Dad were probably enjoying the quietness, maybe they forgot about Richard. Mom did check once observing him pushing snow across the driveway. 'He looks' like he is having fun.' Richard's Mother had thought. 'He will be fine. When he is tired he will come in.'

Midnight of a Friday had arrived when Richard decided that he was tired. Dad had left for work over an hour ago. The depth of the cave was a good ten feet deep when the shovel was propped up against the house. Mom was snoring on the couch. A black and white movie played on the static filled television screen which reminded Richard of the storm blowing outside.

Sleep came quickly after short dreams of continuing to dig a fort into the snow drift on the next morning. Before total sleep Richard hoped that the storm would linger over the whole of the weekend. There was a certain solitude that he enjoyed during a storm.

To Richard's delight the storm had lingered blowing in bursts when he looked out of the kitchen window. His basement window was buried beneath six feet of snow. A quick breakfast of oatmeal then he headed out into the winter wonderland. Dad had arrived home from his eleven to seven shift and already the station-wagon's tire tracks were filled with snow.

First things first, Richard cleaned the driveway before working on his fort. His fort was the biggest and best fort on the street, but no one would see it. It seemed that all of the kids on the street were hibernating. Over the days and weeks of winter Richard worked on his fort. Candles illuminated the darkness within. Benches of snow, doors of snow and rooms of snow. There was no end to the fort in a boy's imagination. It was a winter of self examination of his own mind and abilities. Richard did not miss out on the joys of winter.

Like all things that come to pass winter turned into spring. Overnight it seemed that the fort was there then it was gone. This year of winter storms on Roosevelt Street Richard knew he had the best and biggest of forts a kid could have. His friends were the ones that missed out on the fun to be had in winter.

FORTS
CHAPTER 18
UNDER THE BRIDGE

What makes a kid's mind work? How do thoughts enter? Francis had thoughts in his mind. Brother Terry was a couple of years younger, he was Richard's age. Francis seemed short and stocky while Terry was more lanky and on the skinny side. Like younger brothers, Terry followed Francis around. That would mean he was there when Francis got his ideas.

Francis was not overly tall or big, but to younger kids of twelve he seemed big. There are kids, when one looks at their persona, reflect what type of work they will be doing when they get older. Francis looked intelligent, a thinker, a shirt and Tie type of worker. As a kid Francis did kid things, getting gritty, working in mud and getting his hands dirty.

It was when a kid becomes an adult is when one wonders why certain events occur during the kid years. Sitting here now I wonder why Francis started an excavation. I did not know then nor do I know now. As a kid Francis did it for the sake of doing it.

"Francis! Where are you going?" asked Terry. "Where are you going with dad's shovel?"

"Do you need to know about everything I do?"

"Yeah."

Francis gave a sour looking sneer towards Terry. Taking a round mouth shovel from the back porch, Francis headed out of the door. Almost stepping on Francis's heals Terry escaped through the screen door before it slapped back against him. This time it did not snap back, Francis had pushed the door too far for the spring to work.

There were no soft closing cylinders on doors. No normal kid would softly close a door behind himself.

Terry's mother yelled from another part of the house. "Close that door, you are letting the flies' in."

Looking back into the doorway that lead into the darkness of the porch Terry paused to think things over for a moment. "If I leave the door open for a while why won't the flies just fly out."

"Close the door!" came Mother's final warning.

A swift slap of Terry's hand added momentum to the mighty spring clipped to the centre of the door. Fathers tend to over do a repair job when the wife of the house complains relentlessly about a minor irritant.

"Do not slam the door needlessly!" Mothers' words echoed from every window of the house.

Terry did not wait to look into his mother's eyes, he hurried hotly onto Francis's path leading away from the house. Just at that moment Mrs. Hebert leaned out of the upstairs window.

"Do not slam the screen door!" trailed Mrs. Hebert's voice as she eyed her young daughter emerging through the flimsy screen door. She knew that the cause of the slamming was not caused by her little girl. Drawing her head back into the room, she commenced to tidy up the girl's room. Suddenly little hairs arched on the back of her neck. Again the bang of the screen door bounced against the door jam. Mother just mumbled under her breath

Little girls always watch and emulate older brothers. What Terry picked up from Francis was passed onto their baby sister, she had learned well.

Every house had a screen door with the constant buzz of house flies trying to get in and an equal number trying to get out. Husbands that dabbled in the art of inventing applied and redesigned an assortment of door closures. All were guaranteed to work until they were time tested by kids.

Rubber tires cut into strips and nailed to stretch from door to frame. A rope, a pulley and a weight strung from door to header then to a weight levered the door closed. Coil springs of all diameters and lengths were used. Mr. Herbert and thought he had solved the problem by installing a one inch diameter stainless steel coil spring twenty inches long, twenty inches when coiled closed.

There was plenty of tension and when it worked it pulled the door closed with power and speed. How could a wife nag about such efficiency? All foolproof applications soon faltered when kids forced doors open beyond normal. Though the spring was good, its only flaw was that it could be stretched four times its closed length.

When the spring worked it would work well. Only the sound that it made when slamming closed gave a new item for the wife to point out to her dumbfounded husband.

□□□□

Francis and Terry were well out of hearing range of the slamming screen door. Cutting through the back property lines, between the houses facing Roosevelt Street and those facing Whitney, both brothers were near the creek. This same creek that crossed Second Line, the same one that held the swimming hole. Flowing south the creek headed towards Roosevelt Street then abruptly turned and headed towards Whitney Street. There at Whitney the creek crossed under a five-ton maximum weight timber bridge. Francis and Terry followed the winding creek towards the bridge.

Timber two-feet square spanned the creek. Pillars just as thick were pile driven into the earth at the sides of the creek. Full two-inch by six-inch planking covered the beams. Sunlight peeked through the spacing between the planks. On a hot summer day when it was blistering hot it was cool beneath the bridge.

Terry stepped into Francis's footprints in the sand banks of the creek. "Where are you heading Francis?" asked Terry of his silent brother.

"I will show you." answered Francis without slowing his pace. "But you better not tell anyone."

"Tell what, I do not know where I am going or what you are going to do." Terry shook his head back and forth. "Why are we following the creek?"

Francis stopped in the mid of a stride. Terry was not paying attention to his surroundings as he bumped into Francis. "Why do you have to ask so many questions?"

Terry stepped back as Francis turned to face him. Shrugging as he thought, he answered. "If I do not ask, I will not learn nothing."

"Anything. I will not learn anything."

"Right, so I need to ask questions."

Francis turned into the direction of the bridge nodding his head in agreement of Terry's statement. "Just do not ask too many questions at one time."

"How many should I ask at one time?" Questions seemed to be called for. "What if I need to know more than just an item?"

Francis did not answer for obvious reasons, he knew he would have to answer eventually. "Quiet, make sure no one hears or sees us." Crouching down, Francis looked from the bushes to the road fifteen feet above their heads. "There is no one around, follow me."

Terry followed step by step behind Francis from the bushes into the darkness under the bridge. Clear water cresting over rocks echoed from the eastern fur and hemlock structure of the bridges' belly.

"Did anyone see us?" asked Francis. Terry's head pivoted from side to side then he strained to look up through the slats of the planking. Without warning a car passed overhead with its tires making a flap, flap sound against the ribbed surface of the bridge. Terry's hands raised to cover his ears. Sprinkles of fine dust danced through the beams of light.

"So Francis, what are you going to do with the shovel?" Terry asked while his hands waved through the floating dust.

Francis pointed up towards the pillars placed deep into the bank. "See up there, that hole."

A nod confirmed that he had. "Yeah so what, it is a hole."

"Use your imagination. In behind is an ideal place to dig a fort!"

"A fort underground?"

It did not seem like an ideal place to have a fort. Who would want to live like a mole? Terry showed an unimpressed face towards Francis's idea of accommodations.

"Who will want to live underground?" inquired Terry, squinting his face comically like an out of work clown. "It looks spooky."

"That is what will make it a great fort." Francis began to get excited with his explanation to Terry. "It is well hidden. No one in their right mind would want to stick their head into a dark hole." Francis climbed up the gravel bank to point at the hole. "See, the entrance is small. Inside there is plenty of room. From that end to that end we can dig out and dig as deep as we like." With outstretched arms Francis dramatically exaggerated the fort's dimensions.

"Who is going to dig out this fort? Who is going to do the crawling in?"

Francis disregarded Terry's multiple questions. Maybe he did hear then decided to continue with his own ideas before entertaining questions from his kid brother.

"Did you know that prisoners of war use to try to escape from interment camps by digging tunnels under ground? They worked by candlelight. I will get some candles. Prisoners did not have shovels, they dug with bare hands sweating to sheer exhaustion in cramped little tunnels."

Terry listened as he usually did during a boring class in school, his eyes wandered, legs danced, hands were catching invisible specks of dust.

"You sound like a teacher. Is that what you want to be when you are older?"

"Digging day and night. Escape and freedom was the only driving force in their minds." Francis gripped the handle of the shovel with determination of a prisoner of war.

War is sometimes portrayed as glamourous. Even in a state of despair a moment of hope is exaggerated to heroism. Many fathers on Roosevelt Street served in the armed services. There were stories, mostly fabricated, told by sons and daughters about their fathers. It was hard to tell which part was true and which part a son told to build his father up as a hero.

It did not matter, the fact was that each and every person that served for their country was a hero. Fathers lived like heroes in their children's minds. But few fathers elaborated on their personal experiences. Sorrows, hurts and pains of their experiences were kept bottled up inside, a personal demon.

"Dad was in the war."

Terry's legs stopped dancing, hands stiffened, eyes focused on the dark shadow of Francis standing with a hand on a shovel. Suddenly Terry's thoughts were transformed to the war ravaged lands of Europe. Francis resembled his dad when he was young. Dad was in the war. Did he try digging out of a prison camp, was he on a battle field?

"Did Dad have to shoot anyone?" whispered a soft hesitant voice. His young voice was dampened by the constant sound of clashing water over the rocks in the creek bed.

Without interruption Francis continued on with his story. "He must have been in the thick of the fighting, bullets whizzing by, bombs exploding lighting up the night like hundreds of lightening bolts." On a dramatic pulse Francis paused, his voice became somber and low. "Dad never talks about any of that war stuff. I wonder what he did in the army?"

"Who is going to dig out your fort?" Terry brought Francis back to the reality of being a kid on a childhood mission. "I ain't going first into that small hole."

"I will, first the main entrance has to be enlarged then the main area needs to be expanded before moving in. There will be only room for one person inside at first. You will be outside, you have to kick the dirt away to make it look even. We do not want anyone to notice what we have been doing."

Once Francis started rambling on about his plans, it was hard for Terry to interrupt. Not that he wanted to ask further questions.

"We do not want anyone else to know about this fort. If there are too many people, then there will be too many bosses and not enough workers."

"Francis?"

"Make sure you do not tell anyone, no slip of the tongue."

"Francis?" Terry interrupted again.

"We do not want five hundred kids around."

"Francis?" Terry's voice rose above that of his brother.

"What?"

"Finally." said Terry with a whisper that Francis did not hear clearly. Terry knew better than to say the wrong things too loudly, he did not want his ears boxed in. "Are we going to start digging soon?"

Francis paused with a thought that his brother Terry some how was telling him to shut up and get to work. Looking at Terry, who was avoiding Francis's stare, Francis decided to put him to work.

"Take this shovel and start to dig all of the dirt out around those pillars. Make it look like a shelf." Francis handed over the shovel. "I will start on the opening."

With effort Terry began to shovel away the loose dirt then started to level an area into a walk way. By the time the walk way was taking shape, Francis was headlong into a dark cavity. Legs from the knees down stuck out of the hole. When the last of the day's rays of sunlight cast tree shadows over the bridge, it was time to go home.

For the boys this was an adventure in labour that was fun. Take away the self indulged fun, then child slave labour is what had occurred in many cultures in the past including the present. Fun is what a child needs to have in order to grow into an adult.

Each day the brothers snuck off from home to work on their fort. By the week's end somehow there seemed to be an extra kid checking out the excavation. Terry had not told anyone yet, but if Francis broke the rules then why not him. By the first of the week after a weekend of rain there were six kids working on the fort.

The flowing creek had raised in height under the bridge. One had to hang onto a beam support and swing in under the bridge to a landing Terry had fashioned into the earth. Candles lit up the insides of the fort where kids worked squaring off walls and leveling off the floor. Scrap wood from the odd boy's home were fashioned into benches and a crude table. Francis's secret fort was now known as a social club for the neighborhood.

It was Jerry that had told Richard about the fort that he had heard about. Terry met Jerry and Richard at the entrance and invited them in for a visit.

"You can come in and look." said Terry with an apologetic tone to his voice. "But right now it is pretty crowded."

"That is okay." Jerry said as he stuck his head into the dim candlelight glow. "Is there any-more room in here?"

"Room for one." echoed a voice from the bowels of the earth.

"Do you want to take a look Richard?" asked Terry.

"I kind of like it out here. Too many people inside. Sure, I do not mind just a look." Richard leaned his head in far enough to have a panoramic view of Francis's fort.

It was more than a fort, it was a hideout, a place for young boys turning into teenagers to sneak the odd beer and cigarette. A game of poker occupied the table. After awhile Terry gave up life of maintaining the entrance to the fort.

Those that enjoyed the male bonding atmosphere of the fort lingered around until the cold of September chilled the ground. October found the underground fort abandoned.

It was in the following spring that road crews discovered a sinkhole starting to open up at the gravel leading onto the bridge. High water and a recent down pour of rain was officially named the cause. Francis and other older boys from Roosevelt Street found another place to indulge in their past time.

COWBOYS
CHAPTER 19
RODEO

Growing up in the late fifties and early sixties a boy's heroes were cowboys. Oh there were the odd creature features with a green reptile from a swampy lagoon, or a Martian in a simple animated flying saucer. There were no high quality productions then as there will be in the future. Back then we had real men of the sage, cowboys, horses and live rodeos. Heroes like John Wayne, Randolph Scott, Roy Rogers and Jean Autry blazed across the silver screen to tantalize the minds of make-believe.

Kids of Brookfield subdivision were not city-raised, but then again, they were not country folks. Somehow they were stuck in-between two different mediums. Close enough to the niceties of a city where everything was clean and organized. Yet the freedom of walking in nature and smelling the scents of farmed fields was just outside of the back door.

Jerry, Mark and Richard took a step into the west side of their neighborhood. Long gravel roads lead past tall skinny farm houses at the ends of long driveways. One would take a deep breath and savor the different smells of farm life. Sweet smells of green oats, an aroma of a pungent pig sty, a whiff of a sweet and sour manure pile.

"Hey Mark, smell." encouraged Richard. He took in a big deep breath. "Each farm we pass smells different, they have their own aroma."

"Yeah." answered Mark, his two fingers plugging his nose. "Yeah, each one stinks."

"I kind of like the smells." Richard turned his head towards another farm field they were passing by. They headed north on Allen's Side Road. After several short sniffs with his nose in the air, he smiled with a true farmer's satisfaction.

"You guys' ever see a rodeo?" asked Jerry who was ten steps ahead of Richard and Five ahead of Mark. "A real live rodeo?"

"Sure." Even if Mark and Richard had not, they innocently confirmed willfully. "Sure."

Turning to wait for the two slow pokes to catch up, Jerry wrinkled his face as if he were a cowboy staring across a heat-waved desert. "I bet you never saw a real Brahma bull?"

Both boys were unable to confirm with a convincing yes. "Nope."

"I will show you a big mean, long horned, hump backed, a beastly bugger." Sneakers kicked up dust clouds, Jerry waved the followers onward.

Local farms had met their hay-day of producing crops and live stock for local markets. Chain stores were buying bulk from southern markets. Farmers and their sons were taking jobs in the steel mill or the lumber yards. A working farm was a thing of the past. Fields, that were cleared for crop land, were slowly being overgrown on the fringes by natures wild crops.

Some dairy farmers made a strong showing into the seventies. Suddenly ten-fold of dairy farms vanished. A late dairy farmer lingered into the nineties was a rare breed. Earth swallowed fence posts that clung to strands of fence wire. Sometimes bare wire could be seen among the fields of hay. Walking the road towards the Bar X ranch in the early sixties Mark, Richard and Jerry were experiencing the country for the first time.

For a kid, growing up, time is of no relevancy. A kid does not have to be anywhere on time. When the sun first crests the distant horizon a kid is up and at it. Not a moment of the day is wasted. Even with a destination in the mind's foremost thought a kid will always stop to watch a frog dive into a ditch. If a kid is fast with his hands that frog may be scooped up. Several roads away from its birth spot, that frog may travel. Then with no reason, after a close eye inspection, a kid will let the frog jump from his up stretched hand into the cool ditch water. One adventure leads into another, maybe a bee buzzing about some flower needs to be inspected.

On their long walk up Allen's Side Road towards the Bar X ranch, the boys were being entertained by the mightiest of natures small creatures. What kid in his right mind would be board on a sunny September day.

"So what does this mean beastly bull look like?" Mark attempted to casually ask. "Don't all bulls look alike?" Summer enhanced the freckles straddling his nose. Mark never looked like a mean kid. How could a kid with freckles ever be tough looking? "Is someone going to ride this big mean Brahma bull?"

Jerry turned to Mark and walked backwards as he talked. A twitching set of lips was like a poker face, it was hard to tell when Jerry was leading them on. "Some guys have tried to ride this bull.

This Brahma bull is so big and mean that his ugly face will scare a bull rider away."

In the back of his mind Richard searched his memory for an image of a Brahma bull. As if there was a movie projector running back deep in his mind flashing frame by frame of old western movies. Behind soft brown eyes a western frontier unfolded.

Old western movies, for Richard they were not old movies. Because most of the movies were black and white, and television was the same, the movies just looked old. When the chance presented its self Richard would sit on the couch close to his father's arm chair and watch the movies of western wonderment.

At times a glance was cast up to his father. Dad watched the cowboys shoot while riding, then tumble when they were hit. Dad rode his arm chair as if he were that cowboy. There were day dreams in the middle of a movie when Richard transposed his Dad into the old west. Dad would have been a great cowboy.

Frame by frame clicked in Richard's mind. There were long horn cows, short horn, beef, buffalo and milk cows, then the film stopped. There it was, a Brahma bull. Against the grey of a desert frontier a white bull stood on a knoll. Thin hind quarters with massive front quarters accentuated with a huge hump behind a short neck. Loose skin drooped from chin to chest. Mean eyes stared, never blinking, from behind horns that turned inward and down below the haunting eye sockets. What a majestic beast. Any cowboy would stand at a distance to admire. Why would someone want to straddle such a creature for profound enjoyment?

Jerry's voice brought Richard out of his internal movie theatre. "A mean Brahma bull would stomp us right into the ground. There is no way anyone would be able to stay on him."

"Is there anyone there today going to try and ride him?" asked Mark, with an anticipation of hope in watching man face the loss of life and limb to the killer bull. "Can anyone try to ride him?"

"I think you have to be a real bull rider." Richard thought that he was right. "They will not let . . ."

Jerry's feet stumbled as he walked backwards. "I would try. I have seen how the cowboys get on a bull."

"Where?" questioned Mark, trying to call a bluff on Jerry's poker face.

"At a real rodeo." Recovering his step, Jerry began to gesture as he walked forward. "They get the bull into a pen, the cowboy ties a rope around its belly just behind the hump."

Without changing facial expressions Jerry had both Mark and Richard spellbound. Gone from their thoughts were frogs and bees buzzing around roadside flowers. From their master's fields livestock watched the boys pass without an inquisitive glance towards them. With irony it was the cows, horses, sheep and goats that studied the three boys.

"When the cowboy is sitting on the bull's back, he lifts an arm." Jerry raised his arm then nodded his head several times. "At the same time that the cowboy nods his head another cowboy pulls on a rope tied around the bull's waist." Sucking in his stomach to emphasize the strategic area. Jerry continued with rodeo highlights. "That bull goes crazy, jumping, kicking, spinning, spitting and stomping."

Richard and Mark rode the words. After a quick breath Jerry continued."

"If the cowboy does not hang onto the rope with one hand and swing his other he will fall off . . ."

". . . and be stomped by the mean Brahma bull."

Interjected Richard.

Mark followed with his interpretation. " . . . and then gouged by sharp horns." Grabbing at his stomach Mark floundered about the road moaning and groaning with a squeaking kid's voice years away from change.

It was obvious, to all familiar with Jerry's poker face, that at this moment it had disappeared. Both boys had wiggled in on his story. Shamelessly they carried on. Between Marks oohs, ahhs and ouch's, Richard stomped his foot onto the dusty road kicking back loose gravel like a snorting bull.

"It ain't funny." Jerry interrupted the playfulness of boys having fun. "A cowboy could really get hurt real bad, even killed."

Richard locked eye to eye with Mark, both grinned aloof, their eyes acknowledging their success in riling their friend. Mark shoved his hands into his pockets then without focusing glanced into a hay field. Kicking his foot forward Richard's cautious eye questioned Jerry's knowledge.

"What makes the bull go crazy, buck and stomp?" asked Mark. "He looks kind of friendly and gentle when he is standing in a field."

For a long moment the only sound was a long croak of a male bull-frog. Questioning eyes from Richard and Mark made contact. 'Maybe Jerry did not know.' A logical thought in both boys' mind.

Pretending to place both hands on an imaginary rope Jerry yanked backwards as he raised his voice. "Just when they open the gate of the shoot, a cowboy pulls on a rope tied around the hind quarters of the bull." Sucking in his stomach to emphasize the rope's tightness Jerry added. "A loud cow bell is tied to the rope."

Mark produced a pudgy face by blowing air against his inside cheeks. "A cow's bell?"

"I guess bulls do not like the sound of bells." said Jerry with a straight face. "Too much noise."

Why a bull would not like the sound of a cow bell was a great mystery at the time. There seemed to be no basis, no proven facts. No one had ever explained the reason why before. In the movies the cowboys never gave the reason of the cowbell, or why the bull goes wild when it clangs. For boys of Richard and Mark's age, for that matter there was no indication that Jerry knew the true story. Who did know the facts as to why a bull bucks.

Being a cowboy dreamer, and avid fan of cowboy movies, Richard paid closer attention to details when he watched movies. Dad was asked the bull bucking question. For some reason there was no direct answer.

"They just twist and buck." said Fern to his son during a bull riding sequence in an old western movie. "Bulls do not like cowboys on their backs."

"What about the cowbell, Jerry said it was the cowbell." stated a confused Richard.

Dad leaned back into his seat after the television cowboy ate dirt after falling face first into the mud. "No son, it is not the bell."

"I have got to see this bull buck." informed Mark to his buddies. "When do we get to the Bar X."

Jerry pointed down to the curve at the bottom of the hill. "Right there at that creek. Follow the road in a bit and it is right there."

Without provocation the boys began to pick up their pace until they were at a full run heading towards the bottom of the hill. No kid would think of slowing down when they reached the entrance. Arms waving, legs flaying, eyes wide with terror but they did not slow down. Out of control bodies kicked and grabbed at the loose gravel just barely making the turn into the entrance.

Slowing to catch their breath, the boy's eyed their surroundings with wonderment. From an outside world they stepped into a time from the past. Horses of all colours and sizes came and went by with riders dressed in cowboy garb. City slickers tried to mount their steeds. Turning a chestnut head with an inquisitive eye a horse watched a rider use a wrong foot to mount. As if giving a sigh of being impatient the horse faced forward and waited. Eventually a ranch hand helped the rider mount.

Dragging their heels through the mounting area, the boys passed through the old barn. Richard took in a deep breath, that first breath registered in one's mind. Years later an odd breath of a fragrance in the air would set off a reminiscence of a past childhood memory. Oak shavings, bedding, straw mixed with fresh and dry manure gives a sweet smell. Not everyone would agree. Each person has a smell that triggers a feeling, a peace of mind and a longing to be that child taking in that first breath of memories.

Jerry and Mark rushed their visit through the barn. Lagging behind Richard took time to look over every horse. Each horse was looked at directly into the eyes. There was no need to speak. A horse and cowboy have a non verbal understanding, they seem to trust and communicate just by eye contact. Hellos, goodbyes and stories seemed to be exchanged between each horse and Richard. No one would understand if told, unless one experienced the same thought exchange.

Leaving the semi darkness of the barn, Richard stood at the opening of the big sliding barn doors. A satisfied smile covered his face. Without touching, riding or speaking to a horse Richard felt satisfied and pleased with his visit.

By now Jerry and Mark had made their way towards the corral. There at the white fenced corral a crowd was gathering on the bleachers surrounding the oval. Tagging far behind Richard followed stopping at intervals in places that Jerry and Mark had quickly passed by. Richard needed to explore.

Watching several cowgirls making sure that tack was placed properly on their horses, a ten-year-old Richard took mental notes for a future time. In the corral stood three old wooden barrels. With lightening speed each girl rode her horse with agility. Speed against time seemed to be the key when trying to get their horses around the barrels in record time to win.

Through the board fence Richard spotted Mark on the far side standing on the bleachers waving both arms. Mark called out to Richard, anxiety prevailed on his face as he frantically pointed to a pen below the spot where he stood.

White and big. Between the boards the prominent hump of a Brahma bull could be seen. A real live Brahma bull at the Bar X rodeo. Haste is a slow word to explain how fast Richard circled the corral and climbed the bleacher seats to where Mark waited.

Over near the railing of the corral Jerry watched the riders rope caves. It was Mark and Richard who had a fascination with the bull that Jerry bragged about. Sitting as close as possible was a must. If the bull made a move, Mark and Richard would be the first to have a close up view.

Time passed that afternoon as events came and went. In the pen, as wide and long as the beast its self, the Brahma bull stood calmly. Flies buzzed around the moist eyes searching for a landing to take a drink of nourishment. A blink sent flies buzzing. Like a ticking pendulum clock the bull's tail wagged from side to side.

"It does not look mean." Mark informed to his buddy.

"Kind of tired looking." said Richard placing elbows on his knees and resting a chin in sticky palms. "Do you think because he has no horns means that he is not a mean bull?"

"Maybe . . . but it sure does not look mean." Mark followed suit by resting his sunburnt freckled face onto his hands. "Any minute he just may go to sleep."

Hunger pains from a missed supper gnawed at the bellies of the kids miles away from home. Not until they had seen the Brahma bull do his stuff were Richard and Mark going to leave. Events dwindled as fans came and went and ruffed bleacher seats emptied.

Alas the rodeo was over. There was no show of might and power from the big white Brahma bull. All day it had stood in his pen giving no indication that the beast was anything other than a big gentle creature. If in a field of tall grass filled with buttercups he would be gently sniffing each one.

Filled with the displays and excitements of rodeo events somehow the boys were going home disappointed. Walking the long distance home seemed to take longer as the boys shuffled their heavy feet. Silence prevailed most of the way. Richard contemplated the domain of the Brahma bull at the Bar X ranch. Down Roosevelt Street, as the grey of the evening turned to black, Mark's house came up first then Jerry's.

"See you later." said Richard. In the back of his mind he hoped that they would visit the Bar X again. Maybe the Brahma bull would do his best to entertain them.

It took years to figure out the bull bucking secret. After all the thought and study it dawned on Richard that it was not a secret after all.

Reaching puberty gave him his first major understanding when pranksters gave him a wedgie. No bull in its right mind would like his private parts cinched by a rope. Richard did not blame the bulls for bucking and twisting to rid its self of the rider and the cinch belt.

COWBOYS
CHAPTER 20
FIELD OF HORSES

It is not funny to see life change, to see families arriving, then leaving years later. Ancestors came to clear land, raise a family in a house built on a homestead. Years of hard work, through seasons of complaint and wonder, eventually took its toil on the families. Through death or a mutual decision just to live, families moved. Farms dwindled, barns sagged from being un-used and fields only sprouted twitch grass.

Old barns are an explorer's finds of wonderment. A cool August during a summer when Richard and Mark were about eleven years of age. Jerry had discovered three old barns. Where they were was Jerry's secret, he was the only one that could lead them to the old barns.

"When do we go?" Mark asked, pulling his belt one notch tighter. A good foot-long section of leather hung loosely.

It had been a lean summer for the boys. Being on the move from one place to another meant that there was not much time to devour a whole meal. A snack here and there then it was back to discovering and exploring. No wonder a kid would loose weight. A man does have to hold up his pants. Mark added another notch to his belt. It seemed that he was the only one to loose weight.

"Where is this place?"

Jerry seemed to ignore Richard's question. "Over there." he pointed northward towards Second line. "Are you guys ready to go?"

Richard and Mark nodded as they walked down Mark's driveway.

Mark must have finished his lunch as quickly as he could. A milk moustache covered his upper lip. Licking most of it off with his tongue, Mark then wiped the rest off on his shirt sleeve.

It was no use to question Jerry as to where the barns were. Both boys knew they would eventually be shown the way. Afterwards they would remember the directions. Jerry always took the long way around just to try and confuse his buddies, it never worked.

Going exploring was like taking a trip. In order to get to a destination one had to take in certain sights along the way. Even if places had been visited a hundred times during the summer, it had to be visited again. Instead of following Roosevelt Street around to Second Line, the boys crossed the creek at the north curve.

"No fishing today." informed Jerry.

Marked leaned over his knees to peer into the muddy water. "Look at the water walkers."

Who cares about scientific names? A kid calls a bug as he sees it.

"It looks like they are skating on water." added Mark to his observation.

For a moment Richard pondered a thought. "What happens to them when the water freezes?"

Mark answered with a shrug of his shoulders. With inquisitive interest in the water walkers ability, the boys had to venture onto other matters. Jerry tossed several rocks into the water. Each and every water walker scattered for safety. When the water settled, they returned to the same location. Why? Richard questioned his mind before continuing on with the others.

While they made their way across Second Line, past the curve in the creek where the swimming hole was, Richard wondered about his buddies. Everyone has particular habits as a kid. Jerry was never a mean kid but at times he would pull the legs off of Daddy Long Leg spiders.

Mark seemed like the scientist type. At times he resembled an absent-minded professor. When flies became sluggish in cool weather and would land on hands and arms, Mark would watch them. After a few seconds he would shoo them away. Mark told Richard that flies could land on you for just a few seconds, any longer and their germs would stick to your skin. 'People got sick.' Mark would say.

If this is a kid's peculiarity, Richard's was that he observed his surroundings. He was not much of a talker, or over intelligent, some would think of him as boring. Richard studied people, studied things that happened then in his mind asked why? Why this or that, just why, wondering why things occurred and for what reason.

There was no sign that there had been a swimming hole in the bend of the creek. By now the banks had been overgrown. Stopping for a moment the boys eyed the creek. Though it was over a year it was as if the voices of fun and laughter echoed in their minds. Time passes and also the moment, the boys moved onto the next adventure.

Leading the way along side of the creek, Jerry headed towards the Avery property. A culvert bridge crossed the Avery driveway.

Water that was backed up on one side of the culvert then rushed out of the other side foaming into a miniature waterfall. Avery's were a large family dabbling in the trucking and construction business. Most of the land along the creek on the north side of Second Line was owned by Avery family. They owned the Bar X Ranch.

Richard thought about the Brahma bull, wondering if it still resided at the Bar X Ranch. Though the Avery construction business occurred on the property that the creek ran through, it was normal to have kids from all over fishing at the culvert. Mark and Richard watched an old guy fishing beside young kids. Despite the great age difference both acted like thrilled little kids. Anxiety showed on their faces as they each reeled in small speckle trout.

While Mark and Richard watched the excitement of fishing, Jerry talked to friends about the ones that got away. Jerry's hands were spaced a good distance apart. Most likely it was to show the length of a fish that he had reeled in or had to throw back.

"Lets go." called Jerry to his buddies.

Leaving was hard. Mark and Richard were as excited as the fishermen. Both could have stayed for the rest of the afternoon fishing without physically fishing.

"Which way now?" Mark asked with a reluctant voice.

"Through the bush."

"Okay." was what Mark and Richard replied. Both knew they had to follow Jerry even if they knew there was an easier and shorter route to the barns.

A mixture of Avery's discarded trucks and earth movers with the rushing creek disappeared when the boys entered the bush. There was quietness, no longer loud noises, it was as if the bush had put up a wall to block the sounds. Birds and ground squires emitted sounds faintly through the bush.

Emerging from the bush was like entering a picture perfect day from the gloom of the dark ages. Their eyes peered over wobbly fence posts, over hay fields towards three barns that were sun bleached grey. Silently they sat as if they were slowly becoming a part of the earth. Forgotten, left to their doom, no longer needed by farm animals of farmers.

What a great place for a kid to explore. Surely the old barns would be happy to have visitors. Jerry, Mark and Richard would be glad to offer their services. It now was a race across the field of a second growth of hay. No one had to say 'get ready, go', a kid just knows when a race is on.

By half the distance all three were side by side. Mark was lagging at the three-quarter point. Thick growing hay made the boy's legs feel like weights were placed around their ankles. Jerry began to slow as Richard, with his long legs, easily gained. It was obvious by the seven eights distance that Richard would reach the barn first.

It is funny what goes through a kid's head when he is really not thinking about it. Richard was going to be first, the winner. Looking over his shoulder, Richard saw Mark way behind with Jerry pushing to close the distance.

'What good is being first.' thought Richard. What a weird thought to have. 'My best friend is . . . , I will slow down and let him catch up.' Richard's legs slowed without showing Jerry that it was done with a purpose.

"Hurry up." called Jerry, with a burst of speed he passed Richard. Jerry slapped both hands against the barn's planking. A dry rattle vibrated through the entire length of the barn. With legs spent of strength he leaned his back against the wall panting for expired breath. "What is taking you so long?"

"You did not have to wait Richard." Mark slowed to a walk. With both hands he reached for the seed tops of the hay. Drawing cupped hands up the stem the seeds popped free. Unknowingly Mark was sowing wild oats.

Richard pulled a long stem free from its roots. A cool moist end he placed between his teeth. On the first bite cool pulp moistened a dry mouth. "I was in no hurry, the barn is not going anywhere."

Taking their time, Mark and Richard wasted moments talking as they chewed on green stems of hay. By now Jerry had disappeared into the first barn.

"Hurry up." echoed Jerry's voice from the hollowed walls of the barn. "Up here."

How long ago had the sounds of barn yard animals left? Did the barn miss those sounds, sounds of mooing cows, a horse's nay, or the constant chatter of clucking chickens? Only a lone field mouse occupied the barn's crannies. An odd pigeon looked down from the rafters.

Climbing a ladder, just on the in-side of an open door, Richard followed Mark up into the hay loft. Sunlight beamed into the inner darkness. Through the spaces between the barn boards small specs of pollen glimmered like gold dust. The hay-less barn seemed huge to young kids. Beam-less rafters were dizzily high.

Through the open space Jerry was running from side to side. Mark and Richard quickly joined in for the pure fun of just doing it. Skipping, dancing and chasseing each other.

In a moment of watching a pigeon bobbing its head, Richard did not notice Jerry and mark race towards the opposite side of the barn. Not waiting to be left behind he began a slow run down the centre of the barn. Dead centre lay a hay bail and Richard was heading towards it. Just as he took a lazy leap over the bail with his lanky legs a loud voice bounced off of the walls.

"Do not jump!" yelled Jerry from the far end of the barn.

There was a certain feeling of impending doom in Richard's thoughts. Doom that you know is going to happen after you have begun the event. Richard knew he should not have begun his jump over the hay bail.

For that moment, that seemed frozen in time, Richard saw a strange look in Mark's eyes. Jerry's words were clear 'do not jump' but it was too late. Mark's eyes, his brown eyes looked vacant, empty like a zombie, an empty shell of the living dead.

There was all the time in the world allowed for Richard to look from Jerry to Mark then to the emptiness below his stretched legs. Behind and below the bail of hay was a trap door in the floor. Loose strands of hay floated to the ground twenty feet below. How lightly they landed. Richard could not go back to start his jump over. Nothing would change the path of events. No waving arms, no motion of running, nothing.

Thoughts, either past present or future, were not running through his mind. It was as if his mind was pausing as the world around him continued. Richard's body was sailing through the air with the trap door open like a giant mouth ready to swallow a victim. Rubber soles of his black canvas running shoes landed at the edge of the opening. It was a little bit of momentum that carried the body forward. Loose hay acted as lubrication letting the running shoe slide.

A cold flash of anxiety flashed over Richard's body. It was an almost perfect landing. In front of his friends Richard had escaped danger. A lagging toe was the only part of his anatomy to fall below the edge and catch the lip of the trap door.

Mark rushed towards Richard with agitated concern. "You did not know there was a hole there?"

"No." answered Richard, wondering if Mark was able to notice a quivering in his voice. "I did not know that it was there."

At the moment of the jump Jerry was concerned but changed his attitude after Richard cleared the bail of hay and the opening.

"No problem clearing that hole, eh Richard?" boasted Jerry. "An easy jump to make, I would have no problem."

Mark and Richard were no doubt thinking of challenging Jerry with a double dare. While Richard eased his breathing, the three boys stood looking at the bail of hay, the opening and the hard ground below. Jerry did not back up his statement by attempting a jump.

The moment passed as the next adventure began. Boys are not interested in idle deliberations of what-ifs. There were two other barns to explore. Behind the first barn stood a smaller pole barn with its loft filled with loose hay. Who could not resist a mound of loose hay? Like would-be dare devils the boys jumped into the hay. Climbing a ladder to a higher landing fifteen feet up the side of the barn wall, the boys became high divers. Oh the imagination of diving into a pool of water from two hundred feet up on a swaying ladder.

It is funny that at the moment it seemed that the hay diving lasted all day. In memory the play lasted reflected moments. Onto the next barn to explore. It was just the need to see what was there. The needs to climb, dig, discover and conquer. Why? Just because it is there. Things in the world are just there for the simple reason to satisfy the needs of children to climb, dig, discover and conquer.

Up until now the exploration of the barns had revealed nothing. No bones, tools or odds and ends of nothing important, except in the last little barn. It was not much of a barn, more like several stalls sheltered by a barn style roof.

The small barn seemed to be the oldest of the three. Barn board nailed to poles imbedded into the ground seemed to have sunk deeper. It was as if the earth was swallowing the barn. Doors were shorter. One had to bend over to look out of a window frame. Neglect was its demise.

For the boys today, their exploring had revealed nothing of importance until their eyes sighted an old saddle. A single saddle was caked with dust and pigeon droppings. It was not a cowboy saddle, not a real western saddle. Just the same, the English style saddle did gather the boy's interest.

Each taking a turn they mounted the cleaned off saddle. Beneath them was a steed in the form of a weathered horse chewed log. Boy, did they ride that steed. Each riding in their own dream. Was it a horse race, riding the lone prairie or being tossed by a bucking horse?

Black leathers squeaked with stiffness, a lack of oil and of use. Sitting in the saddle, even though it was an English saddle, was exciting. What the boys wanted was a real horse beneath the saddle. Soon this excitement faded. It was time to mosey on home and for a tired cowboy supper.

Slowly staggering aimlessly across the field the boys noticed a herd of horses in a field two-sections away. Up to forty horses, of different colours and sizes, were silhouetted against darkening skies. Peaceful and calm they seemed to be until the boys placed their feet onto the square boxed steel fence. Rusting steel wire squeaked against dry cedar fence posts. Like a vibrating piano wire, with an off key pitch, the sound echoed from post to post.

Silence was cut by the sudden high squeak. Horses ears perked straight up, neck mussels tensed and eyes rolled. Thunder without clouds and lightning echoed as the horses stampeded in unison. Through the ground a low rumbling began with horses hooves pounding the hard clay-based earth.

Standing up and leaning against the fence wire, vibrations crawled up the fence post then along the wires. Within their chest they could feel the thumping of horses hooves. An intimidating sound. This was an introduction of the power of nature, the boys were willing students.

With wonderment the boys watched the horses run wild from end to end at full speed. In a mass they would slow, some would begin to eat, then a horse would spook and off they would go again.

The sight must have been overwhelming. After stepping to the ground there was still a thudding in their chests. There were no words to describe what each was feeling, there was no need to discuss it. Thrilled, excited and pleased with the experiences Jerry, Mark and Richard headed home. Their minds had affirmed that they would be back another day.

◻◻◻◻

Even a night of anticipation was too long to wait for the next day to arrive. Cowboy dreams drifted through their minds like dry winds across a prairie expanse. Thundering hooves pounded, Richard could feel the vibrations through his body. In the darkness of his basement bedroom, Richard awoke from a ride on a racing horse. The thundering was real, not of horses hooves but of his two younger brothers Donald and Marc playing with toy trucks in the room above. By whatever means the new day had arrived, a new day waiting for the boys to visit the horses.

Those horses belonged to Avery's, who owned the Bar X Ranch and construction company. When not being used at the Bar X Ranch for riding the horses enjoyed leisure time roaming freely on pasture land. Towards the pasture behind Avery's construction site was where the boys were heading. A flutter of excitement beat in their hearts as they walked a step faster up Roosevelt Street. This time Jerry was not going to lead them the long way around.

Stopping at the second line, the boys waited impatiently for traffic to clear. Taking advantage of the last of the lingering warm summer days most of the cars were heading to Pointe Des Chenes park. There on the east shore of lake Superior cool water lapped the sandy beach.

Standing on the south side of Second Line, the boy's interests were on the horses not on swimming. A distinctive smell of French fries and vinegar drifted through the air. In the late morning people could not resist a stop at the "Bob Inn" for fries. A small building with only five booths and stools at the counter served up fries and burgers as the music of the sixties blared from a radio.

'Dream, dream, dream sang the Everly brothers as Jerry, Richard and Mark crossed Second Line to take a short cut through the 'Bob Inn' parking lot. It was as if nothing could side-line their intentions today. Past the fishing hole where friends were, they headed directly through the bush to the pastures behind.

Sure-enough, the horses were there running as one herd. Excitement dwindled when they noticed other kids lining a fence. Several other kids where running wildly after the horses. Some of the kids were not familiar to the threesome. There were kids they knew, Francis, Terry, Tom, Pat, Bill and David.

"Hi." greeted Terry.

"Hi." answered the boys. There were hints of questions in their stares.

"Francis is trying to catch a horse to ride." Terry pointed to his brother running in the field.

Francis was always twenty feet behind the slowest horse. Other kids tried to circle the horses and send them towards Francis. Obviously they were not having much success.

Mark stepped onto the fence. "Terry, how long has Francis been chasing those horses?"

Looking upward to the placement of the sun, Terry determined a time. "All morning."

"A horse bit me." announced a girl from the group of kids. In a flower printed dress, the girl exposed her shoulder and neck. "See!"

Inquisitively the boys looked as did everyone else. It was a badge of courage and curiosity requiring repeated inspections.

"Look at the tooth marks." added Terry as he touched an indentation.

"Ooh." sounded the girl in a low voice.

There were dry tears in her light brown eyes. Richard looked from her eyes to the tooth marks and back. A perfect indentation of teeth circled her shoulder and up the soft tissue of the neck. Bravely she endured the pain and willingly would show the marks again and again during the day. An inspection was required to see if it would go away before she headed home. How would she explain it to her parents?

"I was standing over there." she pointed to where Francis was standing. "One horse went by then turned its head and bit me." Looking towards the herd of multi coloured horses she pointed to one at the lead. "That mean looking dark brown one."

Suddenly the running horses turned towards the kids gathered around the fence. In hot pursuit were Francis, Tom, David and others in a fan pattern. Pulling up her dress strap, the girl crawled through the fence. Terry jumped down as the others backed away. A wave of moving air caressed their faces as the flow of horses flesh stampeded by.

Jerry stepped to the fence to talk to the approaching chasers. "You guys are not having much luck catching a horse."

Leaning against the fence post, Francis draped a length of rope over the wire. Exhausted, the others dropped to the ground without the effort to say hello to their friends.

"Every time that we get close they spook." puffed Francis.

It was Mark that came forward with an idea. "Why don't you, just Francis, sneak up to a horse with a rope hidden behind your back?"

A silence for only a second then everyone began to talk with agreements, disagreements and perfect ideas of their own.

"I know where there is an old saddle." informed Jerry to the boys sitting on the ground. "If we ever catch a horse, we could use the old saddle."

"First we have to catch a horse." demanded Tom's words.

Everyone's head nodded yes. To an observer it would look like a bunch of chickens pecking at the ground. It was true that they had to catch a horse, one that is willing to cooperate.

Lunch time had been missed. No one seemed concerned. For the rest of the afternoon as a warm wind waved through the fields, the older boys tried different strategies of capture. They all failed until it was close to supper time. Maybe the horses were tired of being chased all day, maybe Mark had a good idea.

It was after a short rest when the horses were spread out across the field when Francis made his move. By himself he slowly walked towards a mare. Behind his back was the hidden rope. Being too busy eating, the horse did not bother to move. Maybe it was fed-up with running. Several soft strokes of his hand along the horses shoulder then the rope was placed around its neck.

Too easy, but credit was not given to Mark for the idea. Francis was the hero of the moment as he approached with the horse at his hands. Some horses are willing to cooperate. When they are in a group, they tend to run with the rest.

Excitement prevailed at the fence and loading area. Without a saddle with a stirrup it was difficult to mount the horse. Francis walked the horse around in a circle until he managed to get the horse to stand near the fence. After all those hours of running, chasing, waiting and running the kids had their first chance to ride a horse.

The bigger boys rode alone, the girl that was bitten even rode while Francis walked the horse leading it by the rope. Then the younger ones took their turn. Everyone had a turn while Francis was entitled to rides in between.

Terry looked up into the sky then informed his brother. "Francis, it is getting pretty late. I think it is about supper time."

It was. Most of the kid's bellies confirmed that missing lunch meant that missing supper was not an option. There was a matter of checking in with parents to let them know one was okay. Missing lunch, well a white lie was required. Each kid ate at the other kid's home.

"Tell Mom I am at a friend's place." Francis told his brother Terry. "I am going to stay here and ride."

Some kids were staying, some headed home and some planed on coming back after their meal.

Francis, Jerry and some other kids stayed. Terry, Mark and Richard headed home together with intentions on returning.

Supper time in the neighborhood seemed to be programed. Every mother had the evening meal ready at five o'clock. The Roosevelt kids arrived in time to sit, make an excuse for missing lunch, down their meal then hurry to get back to the field of horses.

Things had changed when the kids began to gather at the fence. Francis had the same horse but the horse had added features. A halter made out of pieces of rope was attached to the horse's head. There, on its back was a saddle, an English saddle. Indeed, the English saddle from the abandoned barn would suffice.

Everyone had a turn at being a cowboy and feeling the might of a horse beneath their legs. A leather smell mingled with the sweat of the horse permeated the warm summer breeze. Late summer daylight hours were now shorter as the sun sank below the horizon earlier and earlier each day.

Under the dim light of evening most of the kids were heading home. Mark and Richard took their leave but not before someone had loosened the saddle cinch. Tom stepped from the fence post onto the horses back then slipped his feet into the metal stirrups.

"Giddy up." said Tom faking an English accent.

After taking several steps the horse stopped dead as Tom and the saddle slipped and rolled under the horse. A turned head from the horse showed dark eyes that seemed to say 'have you had enough?'.

With the daylight hours gone both riders and horse had enough pleasure for the day. Stick shadows of kids made their way home across the field. Against the light grey skies of evening silhouettes of horses moved as patches of dark.

Moments of fun and enjoyment that one thinks should go on forever sometimes abruptly ends. The anticipation of visiting the horses, having a chance to ride again vanished that night. Visiting the various households on Roosevelt Street was Korah townships' constable.

It was a rare visit. In the past there had been no need for a constable to attend a domestic call. In referring to past memory this visit had been the only one. Making his rounds from house to house, the constable was asking general questions, but mostly he was giving a friendly form of advice.

As he put it. "Kids were just being kids attempting to have fun by riding horses. They just happened to borrow an old saddle from an abandoned barn."

Each household, that had a kid that was riding, was given the same little chat. Being from Korah himself, the constable enjoyed coffee from his neighbors.

His explanation continued. "The owners of the horses in question would prefer that the kids not ride the horses in the fields. They are welcome to ride the horses at the Bar X Ranch."

Parents and kids knew that the offer suggested was not meant as free.

"As far as the missing saddle is concerned, I think it will turn up back in the barn by tomorrow morning. That said, I do not think I will be back to enjoy another coffee." said the constable, a pleasant smile on his face.

That was it, no one got into trouble. By the next day the saddle was returned anonymously. In the field the horses enjoyed their pasture undisturbed. Adventure for the kids on Roosevelt Street had to be found elsewhere.

COWBOYS
CHAPTER 21
PEPPER

A door to door photographer, in nineteen-fifty-seven, had to be a sales man, photographer, a horse handler and be patient with kids. How many miles did he walk, how many doors were knocked on? Kids, each family had at lest two to three little ones underfoot. The number of pictures he must have taken in a life time. Earning a dollar per picture was not the way to financial success. His pony alone needed feed, housing and psychiatric help after being subjected to kids.

In the fall of nineteen-fifty-seven a photographer with a pony made his way up Roosevelt Street. From door to door inquires were made. Chances are every kid on the street had their picture taken. At lest every kid that wanted to be a cowboy or cowgirl.

Unpacking his square box camera and film plates from the saddle, the photographer would set up his tri-pod and camera. With uncanny patience his black and white pony would stand still while a kid climbed onto the saddle. Some kids with glee, others with tears and feet kicking while tiny hands cling to their mothers.

When the photographer and pony arrived at Richard's house, when he was five years old, he was ready. This was when Richard lived in the Dewar house up the street. One house before was where Jerry lived, the photographer stopped there then Richard's house then onto Mark's house.

Mom had dressed Richard in a clean shirt, pants and clean buffed shoes. If Richard was going to be sitting on a real horse, he had to have his holster and pistols to be like a real cowboy. Getting up on the pony, which seemed like a towering animal, Richard needed a boost up. Once in the saddle he needed no more assistance, a five-year-old cowboy knows how to pose. With a steady right hand placed on the saddle horn his left hand was casual with a thumb hooked into the holster belt. Cowboys do not smile, they frown with years of determinate hard work. With this look he stared at the photographer and not into the camera lens.

Lifting the black veil of the camera, the photographer peeked through the lens to frame his subject. Satisfied, he inserted the film plate then withdrew the cover to capture horse and rider in a frozen pose. Being familiar with the routine or knowing when to react the horse wiggled his lips into a grin. This was the moment as the photographer clicked the shutter.

Richard sat there in pose waiting for more. To his dismay all that was required was one shot. Standing to the side he watched the man load up his equipment onto the pony.

"I will deliver the picture to you in two weeks Mrs. Mousseau. Thank you."

"Thank you." replied Richard's mother.

Away walked the pony and photographer. Standing with both thumbs hooked into the front of his holster belt Richard reluctantly watched his horse disappear down the driveway.

That era of door to door photography lasted into the sixties. Several years in a row the pony would be seen on Roosevelt Street. Brothers Donald and Marc had their pictures taken on the same horse. Did the horse retire, the photographer or did the industry become redundant? A kid dreaming of having his picture on a horse was devastated with the loss of a traveling horse and photographer.

From the very beginning of growing up on Roosevelt Street every kid lived the cowboy's life. There were no space heroes to emulate, no race car drivers or stunt daredevils in the forefront. No kid would admit that his hero was a singer, politician or even an actor. Hockey players were different, they were heroes only in the winter months.

□□□□

When growing up, a kid only admitted that John Wayne, James Stewart, Randolph Scott, Jean Autry and Roy Rogers were their heroes. Games and toys revolved around the old west of sage brush, deserted dry lands and the majestic emptiness of the mid west.

Mark tried to teach Richard to play chess, it did not work. Eventually when Richard grew older he learned the game of chess. There were cowboys of intelligence that enjoyed the game. Other kids had their secrets of enjoying music, reading, art and writing but no kid even mentioned it outside of their homes.

From the beginning Richard watched cowboy movies and learned from those movies. Pretending with cowboy play with other kids teased the imagination. There was the rodeo at the Bar X Ranch, the field of horses but that was not enough. Richard did no know about the other kids, but he needed more to satisfy a need of pacifying his passion. Richard wanted to be a cowboy.

Turning thirteen years of age seemed to give Richard a new sense of freedom. Mark, Terry, Bart, Billy, Pat and Richard now had the ability to wander further from home. Being the same age meant that there was more to experience. Girls were around but not really noticed by the boys yet. In the sixties, I guess there was no hurry to grow up. Something that is lacking in today's children. As usual, it was the older boys, Jerry, Tom, David and Francis that lead the way into new adventures.

After a summer, that was dry and warm, the weather decided to linger into September. Kids did not want school to interrupt the warm weather that allowed them to pursue their fun.

Boys were sprouting taller, clothes were tight and seemed shorter in the legs. Voices sounded funny as they altered from a high to a lower resonance. Ultimately the boys were changing. The seasons of life were changing. This last summer felt like the last fling of childhood.

On a warm dry Saturday morning on the first weekend of September the boys of Roosevelt Street gathered. Riding bicycles in circles in front of Jerry's driveway, the boys found themselves with nothing of significance to do. It seemed like the first time that boredom raised its ugly head.

Mark, Jerry, Tom, Pat, Terry and Richard circled and rode their bicycles like they were horses. Rearing up on back wheels, spinning they jumped over and through ditches.

"I wish these were real horses." Richard dreamed out loud.

It was the spark needed to set a direction for entertainment,

Jerry reared his bike in front of Richard as he slammed on his breaks. "The Circle Eight Ranch."

"What is that?" asked Richard with renewed excitement. "Where is the Circle Eight Ranch?"

Suddenly without provocation the horse play had stopped. Bikes and riders gathered at the centre of the road, everyone's attention and curiosity had been stimulated.

"The Circle Eight Ranch is over on Korah Road." Jerry said matter-of fact. "I was there this summer with a cousin of mine."

Jerry had been horse riding and did not tell anyone. Richard seemed a little disappointed, after all Jerry and Richard had been friends that summer. Jerry had spent time out at the Mousseau's summer camp. Had Jerry not thought that Richard would be interested in horses.

"It is only fifty cents for a trail ride." Jerry now seemed to be bragging. "I had the same horse three times in a row."

Before a decision to go had ever been made, the boys were digging into their pockets for loose change. Richard and Mark looked at each other, both knew they had nothing in their pockets, there was no need to check.

"Richard, I have some money in a bank at home."

"Good idea Mark, I have a bank with money too."

"Are you guys ready to go now?" asked Tom of the excited boys. "I am ready."

On the spot, in the moment, the boys had decided to go horse back riding at the Circle Eight Ranch. Anticipation of excitement began to serge through the veins of the boys. For the moment boredom had been cast to the depths of the earth.

"Meet back here in ten minutes." said Jerry, giving a time limit for the other boys. "If you ain`t here we are leaving without you." Chewing on his lower lip as he often did, Jerry wheeled his bike in the direction of his driveway.

Departing at full speed, the boys headed home to inform parents of their departure. Change money was acquired by retrieval, borrowing or breaking into the toy bank. Time was a matter of importance. None of the boys wore watches except for Mark, he was the only one that had a Time-x watch. The ten-minute limit did not have any importance. Boys did not need to tell time, they were not concerned about the limits or the duration of time. Events lasted as long as it lasted.

When someone said to meet back here in ten minutes, it meant hurry up and return. Richard now lived the furthest down the street after moving three years earlier. At full speed bike and rider sped along the gravel road that had oil spread over the top to keep the dust down. Looking both ways at the intersection of Roosevelt and Balfour, Richard crossed heading down through the ditch and onto the front lawn. Once making the dip and jump, he had to duck under the massive limbs of two Silver Maple trees. Two massive trees stood like sentinels shading the blue house from the sun.

After dropping the kick-stand, to support his bike, Richard rushed into the side door of the house and headed down the stairs to his bedroom. Noticing his mother feeding his baby sister Terri-Lynn, he announced.

"Going riding with Mark, Jerry and some of the other guys."

That seemed to be enough information for the moment. Taking a small tin can from the dresser, that resembled a safe, Richard turned it over. Clanking quarters assured him that there was money to be retrieved. What seemed to be too long, in comparison to the minutes left before Jerry's ten-minute limit was up, Richard began to shake the tin-can loose of its contents. Faster, one then two quarters slipped through the slot's opening. He now had the knack. Eventually several more quarters fell free. Loose dimes were shoved back into the bank for safe keeping. With a palm full of quarters, Richard felt assured he would get a few rides at the Circle Eight Ranch.

"Bye, I am going." announced Richard to his mother and sister. The speed of his departure was too fast, he did not hear if permission had been granted.

Richard's green bike crossed the lawn, the ditch then jumped onto the rough gravel of the roadway. There was no one on the road in front of Jerry's house. A sudden disappointment flushed through his stomach. Was he too late, had the guys left without him? Slowing up his speed at Tom and Pat's place, he was joined by Terry coming out of his driveway. Anxiety left as the other boys began to gather.

"Ready?" asked Jerry.

"Okay, yup, uha." answered the boys.

"Then follow me."

Like a wild bunch of mustang horses running across the pampas, the boys on bicycles followed Jerry. Down streets, across streets and down roads they had never been on before, the boys headed towards the Circle Eight Ranch. Off a side street onto Korah Road they headed past a pond filled with wild ducks and geese. At this time there was no time to stop and observe nature.

Jerry half turned his upper body on the seat of his bike to face his followers. "It is just up ahead."

There it was, an old grey gravel-sided farm house with a small barn standing in the back field. Kids were all over picking out a favorite horse. Corralled horses of all sizes were tied to the fence railings. Horses, and more at every turn. If Richard's heart was beating, surely so were the other would-be cowboys.

It seemed perfect, a ranch with horses standing around waiting for riders. Leaving their bikes against the fence, the boys stepped into the corral area. Once they were past the gate it was like stepping into another era. An earthly smell of manure mixed with straw and dry dirt drifted through nostrils. Richard made sure to take a deep breath. There was something about the smell of a farm that he liked.

Collecting fifty cents from the kids was a young kid of about seventeen years of age. If someone had no horse picked out, he would match the new rider with a horse. Jerry, Tom, Pat and Terry had their horse picked out before they had entered the corral. Lagging behind searching for just the right horse, Richard looked over the various horse flesh as if he were buying. A boy in a cowboy hat and boots brought Mark a chestnut pony. For some reason, they suited each other.

Letting his eyes wander Richard noticed a small horse all by its self standing at a water trough. It was just standing there away from all of the other horses. No one was paying it much attention. Strapped to its back a worn-in brown saddle with an oversized horn beckoned Richard. Maybe it was the colour that caught his eye. No other horse had as nice a colour and pattern dabbled white, grey, brown and black splattered over its body. A pattern of various sized daubs faded down the legs to the hooves that turned to a solid coat of chocolate brown.

"Okay kid." said the Kid in charge. "Did you pick a horse yet?"

Only a silhouette of the boy could be seen when Richard looked up. Blocking the sun was the wide brim of his cowboy's hat. The voice and stance reminded Richard of a lanky Gary Cooper. Oh, if only to have a cowboy hat, boots and blue jeans with the cuffs turned up.

"What is wrong with that one?" Richard asked of the horse standing by the water trough.

The boy shifted his weight from one leg to the other. "Nothing much."

"He is just standing there. He ain`t tied up or anything." Richard tried to be cool as he placed his thumbs into his belt behind his hips.

"That is okay, we do not have to worry about Pepper."

Pepper, the first time the horse's name was mentioned it became etched into Richard's mind. Richard nodded his head as if giving approval of the name.

"After every ride he goes directly to the water trough and stands there." The kid pushed back a dusty hat up off of a sweating forehead. "Dumb horse."

"Is it okay if I ride that one?" Hope hid behind Richard's eyes. All of the other horses were being taken, no one seemed interested in Pepper. For several seconds Richard and Pepper stood side by side collecting an intimate quiet moment. Two of a kind, they suited each other.

The kid shrugged his shoulder and nodded approval, letting Richard know that the horse was his to use.

"I like this one."

"Okay kid, get on your horse, we are ready to leave." Turning to walk away the Kid called back to Richard. "You have to pull hard on the right reins to make him move away from the trough."

With a side movement of his eye Pepper watched Richard approached and stoke its neck. Just eye contact was enough of an introduction. With a running shoe firmly in the stirrup and both hands on the horn, Richard hauled himself into the saddle. Just like a real cowboy he swung his right leg over and eased into the seat. It was meant to be, the stirrups were the right length. Sitting in the saddle was relaxing, no sign of nervousness. Pepper stood there as relaxed as his rider. It was not a feeling of power of man over an animal, a sense of mutual understanding prevailed.

Oneness until Richard pulled on the right rein. Oiled leather stretched its fibers against the swivel bit resting loosely in Pepper's mouth. Pepper had no intention of leaving his cozy spot at the water trough. Cool spring water rippled from a drip, drip, drip from the tap spout.

Looking over his shoulder at the assembled horses and riders ready to set out on the trail, Richard sighed. Slumping in the saddle he waited while Pepper decided to take one last drink of water before departing.

"What?" as if asking 'what is wrong with you?', Richard glanced from Pepper to the last horse's tail leaving the corral.

Disappointment reflected on a kid's face. All of the disappointments accumulated from a child's past. Richard gave a weak heal-kick to Pepper's right flank. A last slurp, slurp sound echoed as water dripped from the horses lips. One last slurp was taken before the last horse vanished around the corner, Pepper eagerly followed.

Being last out of the corral did not bother Richard, it did not bother Pepper at all. Being content was plodding along ten paces behind with its head and eyes hung low. Richard kind of liked the slow pace, 'pulling up the rear' as they say. Except for the whiff of fermenting gas that the horses expelled. Then again it is what is natural in nature.

From last in line, Richard was able to see the scenery. Perched on tree limbs birds and squirrels watched Richard watch them. What joy of moving in rhythm with a four-legged beast. Now feeling that rocking motion he placed a rein hand on the horn, his other rested on his hip bone. Richard now shared the experiences of his cowboy-movie heroes. Cows, the only missing ingredients were the cows to herd into town after months on the trail.

Last in line Richard let his mind's thoughts wander freely. Far from his mind were city streets, school and other uninteresting parts of life. Maybe he was born in the wrong century. Somehow there was a feeling that he was wearing a cowboy hat, boots and spurs that jingled a soothing tune.

"Hey, slow-poke!" called out Jerry trying to gain Richard's attention. "Mark." added Jerry. "Do not loose Richard on the Trail."

Mark turned a head over his shoulder to look at Richard lagging behind. Giving only a wave, Mark turned back to attend to his riding. Though Richard was looking forward at the moment, he did not hear Jerry's words or see Mark's wave. Pepper and Richard were content to be in their own dream world.

Time seemed to have no limits while the troupe of would-be cowboys wandered the bush trails. Horses stepped over logs, walked through a creek then zig-zagged up a rolling hill.

When Pepper stopped at a clearing behind the rest of the stopped horses, Richard awoke from his fantasy dream. From the clearing on a hill the west end of town could be seen. Tall smoke stacks of the steel mill were touching the skies at the south east end of Bay View subdivision. The scene was unwanted, it was not part of a western movie dream.

Turning his horse to face the others the Kid gave instructions. "We are almost at the end of the ride." With one hand he removed his hat and wiped sweat form his forehead onto a shirt sleeve. "Those that do not want to race down the hill to the barn can go on first."

Kid's eyes and heads peered down the sand hill. Straight down, the hill seemed too steep. A dip was at the bottom where the creek crossed then a small mound before the trail lead into the corral. Not one kid looked into the face of another. Not one kid asked a question or volunteered to be a sissy and walk his horse down the hill.

"No one wants to walk down?" asked the Kid, placing his hat tightly onto his head.

Richard took a good grip of the reins in his right hand then moved his left close to the saddle horn, just in case he had the need of support. A real cowboy would not hold on. With the way Pepper moved maybe the horse would disappoint Richard and walk down the hill after the other horses raced at full speed down the incline.

Mark caught Richard's eyes as he tensed up and clutched both hands onto the saddle horn. Richard took the hint and gripped his left hand over his own saddle horn.

"Are you all ready?" The Kid turned his horse into the homeward direction then slapped the horse's rump with the reins. "Let's go!"

In a thunder of stomping hooves, throaty sounds and yelps from riders the horses were off. Ponies, small horses and big horses vied for position. All ten horses left the level lip of the hill to plunge downward towards home.

Jerry and Tom were on full size horses, Mark held his own on a pony, Terry, Pat and Richard were riding small horses. It was neck and neck at the top then the taller horses pulled ahead. Pepper headed out last as expected. By half way down the hill Richard was hanging on tightly with his legs. A rhythm with the horse was not synchronized yet as Richard bounced against the hard leather of the saddle. At every bounce his legs would slap at Pepper's sides making the horse go faster.

Pepper passed Mark then Terry's horse, Tom was way out in front bouncing his butt clear off of the saddle. Tom's blonde hair floated in the air. Brother Pat with his own silky hair was right behind swaying from side to side fighting to stay in the saddle.

It seemed that Pepper had saved his energy for the past push, a good ploy. Pepper was gaining on Jerry's dark brown horse. Those long horse legs made no difference to Pepper. After each bounce Richard's legs tried to tighten around Pepper's sides. A man's vulnerability was becoming a concern to Richard as his groin landed then slid forward in the saddle. Pounding with every step of the horse's hooves vibrated through his body. Richard had no concern of falling from his horse. He was acutely aware of the need to pee but not while riding. Holding in tension on his bladder and holding onto the saddle horn was enough to concentrate on. Leaving Pepper to the thinking about running was fine with Richard.

By three quarters of the way down the hill Pepper was holding his own position in the race. Pepper was neck and neck with Jerry's horse and ahead of the others. Only Tom, Pat and the Kid were out ahead. The last stretch across the creek and Jerry's horse with its long legs jumped ahead cutting in front of Pepper. What a race, what a rush of adrenaline through veins of both horse and boy.

At the corral the horses gathered near the rail where hay had been waiting. Only Pepper decided not to join the bunch. Regardless of how hard Richard pulled on the reins to turn Pepper he headed for the water trough. Resting in the saddle Richard calmed down as his horse sucked in water. Letting the rains loose Richard took in deep breaths of satisfied pleasure. Beneath his legs, Pepper's ribs rose then fell as he continued to drink.

Dismounting, Richard stood beside Pepper waiting. From behind, the Kid approached to dip a hanky into the water. "You do not have to tie pepper up. She will stay here and wait for his next ride."

"Why do you call it Pepper?" Richard asked hoping it was because of her speed.

"Ever since we got him, he just drinks, drinks and drinks. We thought he was as hot as pepper and needed to drink to cool himself off, so we called him pepper."

Richard stood by Pepper for a moment after the Kid left. Watching him drink, he patted a sweat-covered neck.

"Thanks for the ride Pepper."

The boys had no intentions of leaving, they paid fifty cents twice more to head out on the trail. Each rider selected the same horse. For Richard it was the same routine as the first time. He did not mind. Pepper and Richard understood each other.

That September the boys revisited the Circle Eight Ranch. It seemed like a last get together for the boys as a group. Through the winter and the next year the boys seemed to drift apart as if a phase of life was ending. Everyone was seeking their own interests, goals and paths in life.

It is the fun part of life that one remembers as worthwhile memories. Foremost is a childhood memory of growing up with friends and neighbors of Roosevelt Street that are worth remembering.

ROOSEVELT STREET
CHAPTER 22
ROOSEVELT AVENUE

Not much has changed on Roosevelt Street, except that the city upgraded the road's title to an Avenue. It is Roosevelt Street that holds a lifetime of my memories. Roosevelt Street was just a name of a street where families lived and children grew up. A few more houses were built, families moved away and some stayed. New families moved in, they are another generation, but they are not the same as those that once were.

Houses are neater, lawns are nice and green, saplings are now sixty-foot trees. Fences and hedges divide home owners' properties. Gardens, chickens and rabbits are few. Asphalt covers the gravel road, the ditches are as deep as I remember. There are, at this moment of writing, familiar people still living on Roosevelt Street. All of the kids are gone, some have come back to visit or buy their families' homes.

Those childhood memories are still strong in one's mind. Each kid's face is frozen in time. Pleasant waves and hellos are exchanged, some faces are recognized as others are not. It is sad not to be remembered after spending a childhood growing up and playing together. With the times of today, fast lives and everyone in their own little world, it is possible that some have passed away unknown to others.

At the time of this writing and driving down Roosevelt Street I take note of the family names that still grace Roosevelt Street. Tuning off of a now busy Second Line I notice the same houses and spacious lots. The neighborhood seems a little quieter. Houses are nice and clean with manicured lawns, fences, flowers, but no gang of kids playing in the yards.

I wonder where the lives have taken the names of the kids that I remember. In this story I remember where they came from. Homes on Roosevelt Street carry family names that still reside on the street, the Bradley family, Corbett, Redfern, Seccariccia, Pelletier, Thibodeau, Barber, McAuley, Smyth, Wozny, Mousseau, Potoczny, Bender, Clulow, McFarling, Mckenzie, and Burns. Other family names become part and parcel of history, or have continued elsewhere.

I have lived on Roosevelt Street for about forty years, searching I guess for something. Jobs came and went as did time. Well you cannot make time stand still. Life needs to continued on creating new memories and stories to remember.

There is a point in one's time where events need to be applied to paper. For whatever reason, not known, memories need to be remembered and recalled. I am glad I have these memories to jot down for those that care to reflect on the lives of the families on Roosevelt Street.

THE END

www.ingramcontent.com/pod-product-compliance
Lightning Source LLC
Chambersburg PA
CBHW022024170626
46808CB00003B/1044